FIX-IT and FORGET-IT®
slow-cooker magic

FIX-IT and FORGET-IT ®
slow-cooker magic

Compiled and Edited
by Julie Boston

Oxmoor
HOUSE ®

Fix-It and Forget-It® Slow-Cooker Magic

ISBN-13: 978-0-8487-3231-8
ISBN-10: 0-8487-3231-6
Printed in the United States of America
First Printing 2008

Oxmoor House, Inc.
Editor in Chief: Nancy Fitzpatrick Wyatt
Executive Editor: Susan Carlisle Payne
Art Director: Keith McPherson
Managing Editor: Allison Long Lowery

Good Books
Publisher: Merle Good
Senior Book Editor: Phyllis Pellman Good

Fix-It and Forget-It® Slow-Cooker Magic
Editor: Julie Boston
Project Editor: Vanessa Rusch Thomas
Senior Designer: Melissa Jones Clark
Copy Chief: L. Amanda Owens
Copy Editor: Jacqueline Giovanelli
Director, Test Kitchens: Elizabeth Tyler Austin
Assistant Director, Test Kitchens: Julie Christopher
Test Kitchens Professionals: Jane Chambliss; Patricia Michaud; Kathleen Royal Phillips;
    Catherine Crowell Steele; Ashley T. Strickland; Kate Wheeler, R.D.
Photography Director: Jim Bathie
Senior Photo Stylist: Kay E. Clarke
Associate Photo Stylist: Katherine G. Eckert
Director of Production: Laura Lockhart
Production Manager: Theresa Beste-Farley

Contributors
Compositor: Rick Soldin
Copy Editor: Jasmine Hodges
Indexer: Mary Ann Laurens
Editorial Assistant: Cory L. Bordonaro
Food Stylists: Ana Price Kelly, Debby Maugans
Photographers: Mark Gooch, Beau Gustafson, Lee Harrelson

Cover: Turkey Burritos, page 118
Back Cover: Ratatouille, page 146; Caramelized Pears in Wine, page 51; Tasty Pork Tenderloins, page 23

welcome

Dear Cooking Friend,

My days stay packed with things to do both for my family and my work, but one thing I don't want to sacrifice is putting a heartwarming and healthy meal on the table almost every evening. I bet you feel the same way! If you haven't already discovered the simplicity and versatility of the slow cooker, then you've picked up the right cookbook.

Offering over 200 satisfying dishes with stunning color photography throughout, this is the first hardbound book from the *Fix-It and Forget-It®* authors that offers color photography in addition to the tried-and-true recipes. From appetizers to entrées to ever-surprising desserts, this edition has it all, including tips and hints that will make the slow cooker a busy cook's best friend. Plus there's a special section—15 menus in all—that makes meal planning easy and delicious.

Despite your busy life, you'll easily be able to gather your family and friends around the dinner table every night—thanks to these welcome-home recipes. Pair this cookbook with your slow cooker for no-nonsense cooking. Most of the ingredients you need are probably already in your pantry. And once you've assembled all the ingredients, it rarely takes more than 10 or 15 minutes to get dinner into the cooker. Best of all, the recipes in this collection allow you to fix a meal when it's most convenient for you and forget it until serving time.

With this cookbook, you'll be able to cook, host, and enjoy mealtime with minimal effort. So welcome family and friends home to a treasure of good food with *Fix-It and Forget-It® Slow-Cooker Magic.* Enjoy!

Phyllis Pellman Good

Page 81

Page 138

Page 90

contents

slow-cooker cookbook

Page 65

all about
slow cooking

A slow cooker is a busy cook's best friend. And whether you're
new to slow cooking or have been dubbed a slow-cooking connoisseur,
you'll find these tips and techniques handy.

The Latest Product News

The slow cooker has evolved since it's debut in the '70s. Today's pots are sleek and modern, offering a wide variety of new and updated options. Slow cookers are available in contemporary colors, round and oval shapes, as well as a variety of sizes—from 1 quart to 7 quarts, with half sizes in between. Other extras include an automatic on/off switch, programmable models with digital timers, cookers that can go from the freezer to the oven to the cooktop, and dual cookers that allow an entrée and side dish to cook at the same time. All you need to do is choose the right size of slow cooker for your recipe; many of our recipes list two sizes to maximize your cooking options.

If you're in the market for a new slow cooker, here's an overview of some of today's more advanced products and conveniences.

• Available in 5- and 6-quart sizes, The **Smart-Pot** slow cooker is programmable to cook either 4 to 6 hours on high or 8 to 10 hours on low. Plus,  it automatically switches to warm when the cooking time is done. An added benefit is that the insert is dishwasher safe.

• The **Recipe Smart-Pot** offers programmable settings for temperature and cooking time and stays warm for up to 4 hours after the cooking cycle is  complete. Use your own recipe, or choose from more than 200 preprogrammed recipes digitally stored in the electronic display.

• The **Smart-Set Programmable** slow cooker offers preset cook cycles for foods often slow-cooked, such as chicken, beef, and chili. Choose the setting, and the cooker tracks the food's temperature and knows when it's done.

• The **VersaWare** slow cooker has a stoneware insert that can go straight from the freezer to the oven. You can even brown meat directly in the stoneware.

• The **Cuisinart Slow Cooker** sports a sleek stainless steel exterior and a retractable cord. Handy features include an 8-hour timer, an automatic "warm" setting that is used after cooking is complete, and a cooking rack that accommodates ramekins or other bakeware.

• Some cookers, such as the **Versatility Slow Cooker with Griddle,** now have a base that doubles as a griddle. One model in particular comes with an insulated carrying tote that keeps food warm for up to 2 hours and a plastic cover that makes for easy transporting and storing.

• An **external timer device,** sold separately from your slow cooker, allows you to set the cooking time; when that time has expired, the timer automatically switches the cooker to warm. Simply  plug the timer into the wall outlet, and then plug your cooker into the timer.

New cookers tend to cook faster than older models, so if you haven't bought one in a while, you might want to start shopping.

Secrets to Slow-Cooking Success

• **Use the slow-cooker size specified** by the recipe to ensure proper levels of food, thorough cooking, and safe temperatures. If you do try a different-sized cooker than specified, make sure the level of the food fills the cooker between half and two-thirds full for food safety. Be aware, however, that cooking time may vary accordingly (for example, if using a larger slow cooker, the cook time may be less; if using a smaller cooker, your dish may need more time).

• New slow cookers tend to cook at hotter temperatures than older models. If you're using a new model, **check for doneness at the lower end of the time range.** If your cooker tends to boil contents, check for doneness a little earlier.

• Some slow cookers have hot spots—where one side cooks hotter than the other. If you experience this with your cooker, **rotate the insert halfway through the cooking time.** This technique also allows for even browning of cobblers and crusts.

• Removing the cooker's lid during cooking releases a great deal of heat, so **resist the urge to lift the lid and peek.** Each time you remove the lid when not required, you'll need to increase the cook time by 20 to 30 minutes.

• **Always layer ingredients as the recipe directs.** There's no need to stir the ingredients unless the recipe specifically calls for it.

• Remember that **1 hour on high equals approximately 2 hours on low.** A bonus to cooking on low is that many recipes can cook a little longer than the recipe states without becoming overdone. Avoid cooking recipes with dairy products, seafood, or rice longer than specified.

• **Trim excess fat from meats.** If desired, brown meat in a skillet or a broiler to remove fat and then drain the fat before adding the meat to the cooker.

• Pour liquids over meats, and **use only the liquids specified** in the recipe when cooking roasts and stews. Extra juices cook out of the ingredients and less evaporation occurs than in traditional cooking methods.

• You can **cook cuts of meat that have a higher fat content without additional liquid** when cooker is set on low, though you may prefer to add a little liquid for making gravy.

• **Thicken juices and make gravy** by removing the lid and cooking on high for the last 20 to 30 minutes of cook time.

• We often specify to **cook breads and cakes in a soufflé dish on a rack** in the slow cooker to allow for more even cooking. Add the specified amount of water to the cooker. Let cakes and breads cool for roughly 5 minutes before removing them from the cake pan or soufflé dish unless otherwise noted.

• To avoid soggy toppings caused by condensation dripping into the pot from the slow-cooker lid, **tilt the lid away from the food when removing it.**

• **Stews and casseroles cooked in the slow cooker tend to be forgiving** in how long you cook them, so if you run a little late getting home, you're probably safe.

• Use the warm or low setting on your slow cooker when serving **hot drinks or appetizers.**

Food Facts

• Slow cookers don't brown food, so sear **meats** or **poultry** in a skillet for extra flavor and added eye-appeal.

• Cut **whole chickens** and **large pieces of meat** in half before placing them in the slow cooker to make sure they cook thoroughly.

• Place **vegetables**  under meats in the slow cooker unless otherwise instructed. They often cook slower than meats and, therefore, need direct contact with the bottom and sides of the cooker.

• **Dairy** and **seafood** tend to break down when cooked for an extended time. Unless otherwise directed, add milk, cream, and sour cream during the last 15 minutes of cooking; add seafood within the last hour.

• Fresh **herbs** and **spices** are better than the dried variety for extended cooking times because they take longer to release their flavors. When using dried herbs, opt for whole rather than crushed or ground.

• **Pasta** retains the best texture when cooked separately and according to package directions. Add cooked pasta to the slow cooker during the last 30 minutes of cooking unless otherwise directed.

• **Long grain converted rice** is best in recipes that call for cooking rice in the slow cooker.

• **Dried beans** take longer to tenderize if combined with sugar and acid. To achieve the desired texture, soak beans before adding them to the cooker and add sugar and acid only after beans have cooked until tender.

Slow-Cooker Safety

• **Fill your slow cooker at least half full** but no more than two-thirds full. This helps keep the temperature of the food even.

• Always **cook raw meat and poultry dishes on high for the first hour** to speed up the time it takes to get to a safe temperature. Then you can reduce the heat to low for the duration of the cooking time, if you prefer.

• You can **forgo the high setting for the first hour** if the recipe calls for browning the meat first; pre-cooking jump-starts the initial temperature of ingredients.

• **Defrost any frozen foods** before cooking a dish that includes meat, poultry, or seafood. This ensures that the contents of the insert reach a safe temperature quickly.

Easy Cleanup

• **Allow the slow-cooker insert to cool** completely before washing it. Cold water poured over a hot insert can cause cracking.

• **Never immerse a slow-cooker unit in water.** Simply unplug it and wipe it clean with a cloth.

• **Buy clear, heavy-duty plastic liners** made to fit 3- to 6½-quart oval and round slow cookers. Just fit the plastic liner inside your slow cooker before adding the recipe ingredients. Simply serve the meal directly from the lined cooker. Once the cooker has cooled, just toss the plastic liner. If you're not using liners, be sure to coat the inside of the cooker with cooking spray for easier cleanup.

Once the cooker has cooled, just toss the plastic liner along with the mess.

Page 19

Page 59

Page 23

Page 48

slow cooking
for comfort

the holidays are here

serves 6

Cranberry-Orange Turkey Breast

Elegant Carrots with Onions   English peas

Easy Brickle Cake

Cranberry-Orange
Turkey Breast,
Elegant Carrots
with Onions

Cranberry-Orange Turkey Breast

makes 9 servings
ideal slow cooker: 5-quart

....

½ cup orange marmalade
16-oz. can whole-berry cranberry
   sauce
2 tsp. grated orange peel
3-lb. boneless, skinless turkey
   breast

1. Combine marmalade, cranberries, and orange peel in a bowl.
2. Place turkey breast in slow cooker and pour half of cranberry mixture over turkey.
3. Cover and cook on high 2½ hours or on high 1 hour and then on low 5 to 6 hours until turkey juices run clear.
4. Heat remaining half of cranberry mixture in microwave at HIGH 30 seconds or until warm.
5. Remove turkey to platter and allow to rest for 15 minutes before slicing. Serve with cranberry sauce.

Elegant Carrots with Onions

makes 6 servings
ideal slow cooker: 2- or 3-quart

....

1 chicken bouillon cube
1 cup boiling water
2 medium onions, sliced
1 Tbsp. butter or margarine
1 Tbsp. all-purpose flour
Pinch of salt (optional)
6 carrots, cut into julienne strips
1 Tbsp. sugar

1. Dissolve bouillon cube in boiling water. Set aside.

Whether you're planning a come-as-you-are lunch or a showstopping supper, your holiday entertaining just got easier thanks to the slow cooker. Prepare **Cranberry-Orange Turkey Breast** in one cooker and **Elegant Carrots with Onions** in another. Round out this holiday menu with store-bought English peas and make-ahead **Easy Brickle Cake.**

2. In a large skillet, sauté onions in butter until transparent, stirring to separate rings.
3. Add flour and salt, if desired, to onions in skillet. Add slightly cooled bouillon. Cook until thickened.
4. Stir together carrots and onion sauce in slow cooker.
5. Cover and cook on low 2½ hours.
6. Add sugar just before serving.

Easy Brickle Cake

makes 1 10-inch cake

....

½ cup chopped pecans
½ cup flaked coconut
2 Tbsp. butter or margarine,
   melted
18.25-oz. pkg. yellow or white cake
   mix with pudding (we used
   Betty Crocker)
8-oz. container sour cream
¼ cup water
2 Tbsp. vegetable oil
4 eggs
7.5-oz. pkg. almond brickle chips
1 cup sifted powdered sugar
1½ Tbsp. milk

1. Combine first 3 ingredients; spread in bottom of a greased and

floured 12-cup Bundt pan. Set aside.
2. Combine cake mix and next 4 ingredients in electric mixer bowl; beat on medium speed 2 minutes. Fold in brickle chips. Spoon batter into prepared pan.
3. Bake at 350° for 45 minutes or until a wooden pick inserted in center comes out clean. Let cool in pan 10 minutes; remove from pan and invert onto a serving plate. Combine powdered sugar and milk; drizzle over warm cake.

note:

• To use a 10-inch tube pan, combine cake mix and next four ingredients; fold in brickle chips. Spoon batter into greased and floured pan. Combine chopped pecans, coconut, and butter; sprinkle mixture over batter in pan. Bake at 350° for 55 minutes. Let cool and glaze as directed.

Mexican fiesta

serves 6

Nachos

Marsha's Chicken Enchilada Casserole   Hot Pepper Rice

vanilla ice cream with caramel topping

Nachos

entertaining

Nachos

makes 8 servings
ideal slow cooker: 4-quart

....

Instead of serving this cheesy, beefy spread as nachos, you can serve it as a dip straight from the cooker set to warm, if you'd like.

1 lb. ground beef
¼ cup diced onions
¼ cup diced green bell pepper
13.4-oz. jar taco sauce
16-oz. can refried beans
10¾-oz. can cream of mushroom
   soup
1.25-oz. pkg. dry taco seasoning
   mix
Salt to taste
1 lb. Velveeta cheese, cubed
Tortilla chips
Shredded lettuce
Chopped tomatoes
Sour cream

1. Brown ground beef, onions, and green peppers in a saucepan. Drain.
2. Combine beef mixture, taco sauce, and next 5 ingredients in slow cooker.
3. Cover and cook on high 1 hour, stirring occasionally until cheese is fully melted.
4. Serve immediately with chips, lettuce, tomatoes, and sour cream.

Marsha's Chicken Enchilada Casserole is a meal in itself, but stovetop **Hot Pepper Rice** complements it nicely. If you have a second slow cooker, you can nosh on **Nachos** as guests gather; otherwise, substitute a commercial cheese dip.

Marsha's Chicken Enchilada Casserole

makes 4 to 6 servings
ideal slow cooker: 4- or 5-quart

....

1 onion, chopped
1 garlic clove, minced
1 Tbsp. oil
10-oz. can enchilada sauce
8-oz. can tomato sauce
Salt and pepper to taste
8 corn tortillas
3 boneless, skinless chicken breast
   halves, cooked and cubed
15-oz. can ranch-style beans,
   drained
11-oz. can Mexicorn, drained
¾ lb. cheddar cheese, grated
2¼-oz. can sliced black olives,
   drained

1. Sauté onion and garlic in oil in a saucepan. Stir in enchilada sauce and tomato sauce. Season with salt and pepper.
2. Place 2 tortillas in bottom of slow cooker. Layer one-third chicken on top. Top with one-third sauce mixture, one-third beans, one-third corn, one-third cheese, and one-third black olives. Repeat layers 2 more times. Top with 2 tortillas.
3. Cover and cook on low 6 to 8 hours.

Hot Pepper Rice

makes 6 servings

....

3 cups cooked long grain rice
8-oz. container sour cream
4.5-oz. can chopped green chiles,
   drained
1 fresh jalapeño pepper, seeded
   and diced
4 ozs. Monterey Jack cheese,
   shredded and divided
4 ozs. Cheddar cheese, shredded
   and divided

1. Combine first 4 ingredients. Spoon half of mixture into a lightly greased 1½-qt. baking dish.
2. Sprinkle ½ cup each of Monterey Jack cheese and cheddar cheese over rice mixture in dish. Repeat layers, using remaining rice mixture and cheeses. Bake, uncovered, at 350° for 15 minutes or until mixture is thoroughly heated.

"takeout" at home

serves 6

Chicken Won Tons with Hoisin-Peanut Dipping Sauce
Asian-Grilled Pork Tenderloins
Chinese Vegetables

Chinese Vegetables

Chicken Won Tons with Hoisin-Peanut Dipping Sauce

makes 2 dozen

Peanut oil
1 cup chopped cooked chicken
1 cup finely shredded cabbage
   (prepackaged)
4 green onions, finely chopped
2 Tbsp. finely chopped fresh
   cilantro
1 Tbsp. hoisin sauce
2 tsp. light brown sugar
1 tsp. sesame oil
24 won ton wrappers
Hoisin-Peanut Dipping Sauce

1. Pour peanut oil to a depth of 3 inches into a large Dutch oven; heat to 375° (about 25 minutes).
2. While oil heats, combine chicken and next 6 ingredients in a medium bowl. Spoon 1 heaping teaspoonful of meat mixture in center of each won ton wrapper; moisten edges with water.
3. Carefully bring 2 opposite points of wrapper to center over filling; pinch points gently to seal. Bring remaining opposite points to center; pinch gently to seal.
4. Fry won tons, in batches, 1½ minutes or until golden, turning once. Drain on paper towels. Serve with Hoisin-Peanut Dipping Sauce.

To enjoy the flavors of the Far East, sample these tasty recipes. **Chinese Vegetables** simmer 3 to 6 hours in your slow cooker and **Asian-Grilled Pork Tenderloins** take only a 15-minute sizzle on the grill. The whole family can enjoy wrapping homemade won tons for an appetizer, or you can substitute frozen won tons if you'd rather skip that step.

hoisin-peanut dipping sauce

makes ¾ cup

½ cup chicken broth
2 Tbsp. hoisin sauce
2 Tbsp. sesame oil
2 Tbsp. soy sauce
1 Tbsp. creamy peanut butter
1 tsp. cornstarch

1. Combine all ingredients in a saucepan; bring to a boil. Cook, stirring constantly, 1 minute.

editor's favorite
Asian-Grilled Pork Tenderloins

makes 6 servings

2 ¾-lb. pork tenderloins
½ cup dry sherry or orange juice
½ cup soy sauce
2 Tbsp. brown sugar
1 tsp. ground ginger
2 garlic cloves, pressed

1. Place tenderloins in a zip-top plastic freezer bag. Combine sherry and remaining 4 ingredients; pour over tenderloins. Seal bag; marinate in refrigerator 8 hours, turning bag occasionally.
2. Remove tenderloins from marinade, discarding marinade.

Grill, covered, over medium-hot coals (350° to 400°) 15 minutes or until a meat thermometer inserted in thickest portion of 1 tenderloin registers 160°, turning once. Cut into slices to serve.

15-minute prep
Chinese Vegetables

makes 6 servings
ideal slow cooker: 4-quart

1 bunch celery, sliced on the
   diagonal
1 large onion, sliced
14-oz. can bean sprouts, drained
16-oz. pkg. frozen Asian vegetables
8-oz. can sliced water chestnuts,
   drained
2 4-oz. cans sliced mushrooms
1 Tbsp. sugar
3 Tbsp. low-sodium soy sauce
¾ cup water
¼ tsp. pepper or to taste

1. Spray slow cooker with cooking spray.
2. Combine all ingredients in slow cooker.
3. Cover and cook on low 3 to 6 hours, depending on how soft or crunchy you like your vegetables.

Italian night

serves 6 to 8

Meatballs and Spaghetti Sauce

Caesar Salad   garlic bread

Tiramisu

Meatballs and Spaghetti Sauce,
Caesar Salad

Meatballs and Spaghetti Sauce

makes 6 to 8 servings
ideal slow cooker: 4-quart

1½ lbs. ground round
2 eggs
1 cup fresh bread crumbs
Oil
28-oz. can tomato puree
6-oz. can tomato paste
10¾-oz. can tomato soup
¼ to ½ cup grated Romano or
    Parmesan cheese
1 tsp. oil
1 garlic clove, minced
Sliced mushrooms (canned or fresh)

1. Combine ground beef, eggs, and bread crumbs. Form into 16 meatballs. Brown in oil in skillet.
2. Combine tomato puree and next 5 ingredients in slow cooker. Add meatballs. Stir together gently.
3. Cover and cook on low 5 to 6 hours. Add mushrooms and cook 1 to 2 more hours.
4. Serve over cooked spaghetti.

Caesar Salad

makes 8 servings

1 head romaine lettuce, torn
½ head iceberg lettuce, torn
¼ cup egg substitute
3 Tbsp. olive oil
1 garlic clove, minced
1 Tbsp. lemon juice
½ to 1 tsp. salt
½ tsp. coarsely ground pepper
½ tsp. Dijon mustard
2-oz. can anchovy fillets, drained
    (optional)
1 cup croutons
¼ cup shredded Parmesan cheese

Come home to a classic Italian meal straight from your slow cooker. **Meatballs and Spaghetti Sauce** cooks all day, offering savory flavor with little fuss. Add **Caesar Salad,** garlic bread, and **Tiramisu** for a perfect family dinner.

1. Place lettuces in a large bowl.
2. Process egg substitute, next 6 ingredients, and, if desired, anchovies in a blender. Drizzle dressing over lettuce, tossing well. Sprinkle with croutons and Parmesan cheese.

make-ahead
Tiramisu

makes 10 servings

⅔ cup sugar
3 cups whipping cream, divided
2 eggs
2 egg yolks
1 Tbsp. all-purpose flour
½ vanilla bean, split
16-oz. pkg. mascarpone cheese
¾ cup brewed espresso (see note)
3 Tbsp. Marsala
7-oz. package dried ladyfingers
    (we used Bellino Savoiardi)
3 Tbsp. powdered sugar
1 Tbsp. unsweetened cocoa
    powder

1. Stir together sugar, 2 cups whipping cream, and next 4 ingredients in a heavy saucepan. Cook over medium heat, stirring constantly, 20 minutes or until thickened. Cool completely. Discard vanilla bean; whisk in mascarpone.
2. Stir together espresso and Marsala. Dip each ladyfinger in coffee mixture, and place in a 13- x 9-inch baking dish. Pour cream mixture over ladyfingers.
3. Beat remaining 1 cup cream at high speed with an electric mixer until foamy; add powdered sugar, beating until soft peaks form. Spoon over cream mixture; sprinkle with cocoa. Cover and chill 2 hours.

note:
• To make espresso, stir together 1 cup hot water and ½ cup ground espresso coffee. Let stand 5 minutes; pour through a wire-mesh strainer lined with a coffee filter into a glass measuring cup, discarding grounds. Measure ¾ cup.

company's coming

serves 6 to 8

Tasty Pork Tenderloins

Marinated Asparagus   Grown-up Hot Chocolate

Pecan Toffee

Tasty Pork Tenderloins

Tasty Pork Tenderloins

makes 8 servings
ideal slow cooker: 4-quart

2 1.25-lb. pork tenderloins
1 tsp. salt
½ tsp. freshly ground pepper
12-oz. jar chili sauce
16-oz. can jellied cranberry sauce
2 Tbsp. brown sugar
5 cups cooked long grain enriched
   rice
Garnishes: cranberries, rosemary
   sprigs (optional)

1. Sprinkle tenderloins with salt
and pepper and place in slow
cooker.
2. Stir together chili sauce,
cranberry sauce, and brown sugar.
Pour over pork.
3. Cover and cook on high 1 hour
and then on low 3 hours.
4. Serve over rice. Garnish with
cranberries and rosemary sprigs,
if desired.

Marinated Asparagus

makes 6 to 8 servings

2 lbs. fresh asparagus
¾ cup olive oil
1 Tbsp. sugar
½ cup white balsamic vinegar
4 garlic cloves, minced
1 tsp. red pepper flakes

1. Snap off tough ends of asparagus and cook asparagus in boiling
water to cover 3 minutes or until
asparagus is crisp-tender; drain.
2. Plunge asparagus into ice water
to stop the cooking process and
drain. Arrange asparagus in a
13- x 9-inch baking dish.

What a fast and easy way to welcome company into
your home. **Tasty Pork Tenderloins** go from package
to cooker in seconds while **Marinated Asparagus** chills
overnight, leaving you plenty of time to chat with
your guests. **Grown-up Hot Chocolate** and **Pecan
Toffee** round out this delectable meal perfect for kids
of all ages.

3. Whisk together olive oil, sugar,
balsamic vinegar, garlic, and red
pepper flakes until well blended;
pour over asparagus. Cover and
chill 8 hours. Drain before serving.

Grown-up Hot Chocolate

makes 10 cups

½ cup boiling water
⅔ cup chocolate syrup
8 cups milk
⅔ to 1 cup coffee liqueur (we
   used Kahlúa)
Garnish: whipped cream

1. Stir together ½ cup boiling
water and chocolate syrup in a
large saucepan; add milk, stirring
until blended. Cook over medium
heat 8 to 10 minutes or until
thoroughly heated. Stir in desired
amount of coffee liqueur. Garnish,
if desired.

Pecan Toffee

makes 1¾ lbs.

1½ cups chopped pecans, divided
1 cup sugar
1 cup butter, softened
⅓ cup water
5 1.55-oz. milk chocolate bars,
   broken into small pieces

1. Line a 15- x 10-inch jellyroll
pan with heavy-duty aluminum
foil; lightly grease foil. Sprinkle
with 1 cup pecans to within 1
inch of edges.
2. Bring sugar, butter, and ⅓ cup
water to a boil in a heavy saucepan over medium heat, stirring
constantly. Cook over medium-
high heat, stirring constantly,
12 minutes or until a candy
thermometer registers 310° (hard-
crack stage). Pour over pecans;
sprinkle with chocolate pieces. Let
stand 30 seconds.
3. Sprinkle with remaining ½ cup
pecans. Chill 30 minutes. Break
up toffee using a mallet or rolling
pin. Store in an airtight container
up to 1 week.

simple soup supper
serves 6

Fresh Tomato Soup
Broccoli Corn Bread or Italian Cheese Breadsticks

Fresh Tomato Soup,
Broccoli Corn Bread

Fresh Tomato Soup

makes 6 servings
ideal slow cooker: 3½- or 4-quart

5 cups ripe diced tomatoes (about
    5 medium tomatoes, peeled if
    desired)
1 Tbsp. tomato paste
4 cups or 1 32-oz. container
    chicken broth
1 carrot, grated
1 onion, minced
1 Tbsp. minced garlic
1 tsp. dried basil
Pepper to taste
2 Tbsp. lemon juice
1 bay leaf

1. Combine all ingredients in slow
cooker.
2. Cover and cook on low 6 hours.
Stir once while cooking.
3. Remove bay leaf before serving.

note:

:: • To thicken the soup slightly,
:: you may want to add a 6-oz. can
:: of tomato paste instead of just
:: 1 Tbsp.

If you have two slow cookers on hand, pair **Fresh Tomato Soup** with **Broccoli Corn Bread**. If you have only one cooker, this simple and satisfying supper will be just as tasty with **Italian Cheese Breadsticks** hot from your oven.

15-minute prep
Broccoli Corn Bread

makes 8 servings
ideal slow cooker: 3½-quart round

½ cup butter, melted
10-oz. pkg. frozen chopped
    broccoli, cooked and drained
1 onion, chopped
8.5-oz. box corn bread mix
    (we used Jiffy)
4 eggs, well beaten
¾ cup cottage cheese

1. Combine all ingredients in a
bowl. Mix well.
2. Pour into greased slow cooker.
Cover and cook on low 4 hours for
a spoon bread consistency, or cook
on low 6 hours or until toothpick
inserted in center comes out clean
for a corn bread consistency.
3. Serve like spoon bread, or invert
the pot, remove the bread, and cut
into wedges.

5 ingredients or less
Italian Cheese Breadsticks

makes 8 breadsticks

Dip these pizza-flavored sticks into your favorite brand of marinara sauce.

11-oz. can refrigerated soft
    breadsticks
1 to 2 Tbsp. olive oil
1½ tsp. garlic powder
1 tsp. dried Italian seasoning
1 cup (4 oz.) shredded mozzarella
    cheese

1. Unroll breadstick dough; twist
breadsticks, and place 1 inch apart
on a lightly greased aluminum
foil-lined baking sheet. Brush
breadsticks with oil. Combine
garlic powder and Italian seasoning; sprinkle over breadsticks.
2. Bake at 400° for 9 to 10 minutes
or until golden. Sprinkle with
cheese; bake 1 to 2 minutes
or until cheese melts. Serve
immediately.

make it a sandwich night

serves 8

Italian Meatball Subs
Garden Salad with Buttermilk Dressing
Chocolate Chip Cookies

**Italian Meatball Subs,
Garden Salad with Buttermilk Dressing,
Chocolate Chip Cookies**

Italian Meatball Subs

makes 9 servings
ideal slow cooker: 4- or 5-quart

1 egg, beaten
¼ cup fat-free milk
½ cup dry bread crumbs
2 Tbsp. freshly grated Parmesan
　cheese
½ tsp. salt
¼ tsp. black pepper
⅛ tsp. garlic powder
¾ lb. 85%-lean ground beef
½ lb. bulk pork sausage
15-oz. can no-added-salt tomato
　sauce
6-oz. can tomato paste
1 small onion, chopped
½ cup chopped green bell pepper
½ cup dry red wine or beef broth
⅓ cup water
2 garlic cloves, minced
1 tsp. dried oregano
½ tsp. salt
½ tsp. black pepper
½ tsp. sugar
9 submarine rolls

1. Make meatballs by combining
egg and milk. Add bread crumbs,
cheese, and seasonings. Add
meats. Mix well. Shape into 1-inch
balls. Broil or sauté until brown.
Put in slow cooker.
2. Combine tomato sauce and next
10 ingredients. Pour over meatballs.
3. Cover and cook on low 4 to 6
hours.
4. Serve on rolls.

Reconnect with your family at the dinner table and
enjoy this hearty, home-cooked meal. Kids will love
the saucy flavor of **Italian Meatball Subs.** A green
salad and **Chocolate Chip Cookies** round out this
homestyle and kid-friendly meal.

Garden Salad with Buttermilk Dressing

makes 8 servings

¾ cup mayonnaise or salad
　dressing
½ cup buttermilk
1 Tbsp. chopped fresh parsley
1 Tbsp. finely chopped onion
1 garlic clove, minced
¼ tsp. salt
Dash of pepper
8 cups mixed salad greens

1. Combine first 7 ingredients; stir
with a wire whisk until blended.
Cover and chill 2 hours. Serve
with greens.

Chocolate Chip Cookies

makes 7 dozen

1 cup butter or margarine,
　softened
1 cup granulated sugar
1 cup firmly packed brown sugar
2 large eggs
½ tsp. vanilla extract
2½ cups uncooked regular oats
2 cups all-purpose flour
1 tsp. baking powder
1 tsp. baking soda
½ tsp. salt
12-oz. pkg. semisweet chocolate
　morsels
3 1.55-oz. milk chocolate candy
　bars, coarsely chopped
1½ cups chopped pecans

1. Beat butter at medium speed
with an electric mixer until fluffy;
add sugars, beating well. Add eggs
and vanilla, beating until blended.
2. Process oats in a blender or
food processor until finely ground.
Combine oats, flour, and next 3
ingredients. Add to butter mixture, beating well.
3. Stir in chocolate morsels,
chopped candy bars, and pecans.
4. Shape into 1½-inch balls and
place on ungreased baking sheets.
5. Bake at 375° for 8 to 10 minutes
or until lightly browned. Remove
to wire racks to cool.

a good ole barbecue

serves 6

Barbecued Ribs

Easy Southern Brunswick Stew   Speedy Coleslaw   Texas toast

Cookie-Crusted Blackberry Cobbler

Barbecued Ribs,
Easy Southern Brunswick Stew,
Speedy Coleslaw

Barbecued Ribs

makes 6 servings
ideal slow cooker: 6- or 7-quart
round or oval

....

4 lbs. pork ribs (baby back)
½ cup brown sugar
12-oz. jar chili sauce
¼ cup balsamic vinegar
2 Tbsp. Worcestershire sauce
2 Tbsp. Dijon mustard
1 tsp. hot sauce

1. Cut each slab of ribs into 2 sections. Place ribs in slow cooker.
2. Combine remaining ingredients. Pour half of sauce over ribs. Refrigerate remaining sauce.
3. Cover and cook on high 1 hour and then on low 6 to 8 hours.
4. Reheat remaining sauce to serve with ribs.

Barbecued Ribs tenderize in one slow cooker while aromatic **Easy Southern Brunswick Stew** simmers in another. Both will be ready about the same time with minimal hands-on involvement. Prepare coleslaw at the last minute or make it ahead according to your schedule. **Cookie-Crusted Blackberry Cobbler** is extra-yummy, but if you need to save time, substitute a store-bought cobbler.

1. Place pork in slow cooker.
2. Cover and cook on high 1 hour and then on low 4 to 6 hours. Remove meat from bone and shred. Discard juices.
3. Combine all ingredients in slow cooker.
4. Cover and bring to a boil on high. Reduce heat to low and cook 30 minutes.

Easy Southern Brunswick Stew

makes 10 to 12 servings
ideal slow cooker: 5-quart

....

2 to 3 lbs. pork butt
17-oz. can white whole-kernel corn, undrained
14-oz. bottle ketchup
2 cups diced cooked potatoes
1-lb. pkg. frozen green peas
2 10¾-oz. cans tomato soup
2 tsp. hot sauce
1 tsp. salt
1 tsp. pepper

Speedy Coleslaw

makes 6 to 8 servings

....

16-oz. pkg. shredded coleslaw mix
8-oz. bottle coleslaw dressing
¼ tsp. salt
¼ tsp. pepper

1. Combine all ingredients in a large bowl, tossing well. Serve immediately or cover and chill.

Cookie-Crusted Blackberry Cobbler

makes 6 servings

....

Sugar cookie dough is put to clever use in this recipe to form a crispy dough atop this cobbler.

4 cups fresh blackberries
¾ cup sugar
¼ cup all-purpose flour
1 tsp. lemon zest
1 tsp. fresh lemon juice
9 ¼-inch-thick slices refrigerated sugar cookie dough (we used Pillsbury)
1 Tbsp. sugar

1. Combine first 5 ingredients in a medium bowl; pour into a lightly greased 8-inch baking dish. Microwave at HIGH 8 minutes or until bubbly, stirring once.
2. Place cookie slices over berries; sprinkle evenly with 1 Tbsp. sugar. Bake at 375° for 20 minutes or until golden.

perfect pork plate

serves 4

Perfect Pork Chops

Buttered Green Beans   Chunk-Style Applesauce

Fudge Pie

**Perfect Pork Chops,
Chunk-Style Applesauce,
Buttered Green Beans**

Perfect Pork Chops

makes 4 servings
ideal slow cooker: 3- or 3½-quart

4 small onions
4 ¾-inch thick boneless, center loin
   pork chops
1 Tbsp. hot olive oil
½ tsp. fresh ground pepper or to
   taste
2 chicken bouillon cubes
½ cup boiling water
¼ cup prepared mustard with
   white wine

1. Cut off ends of onions and peel. Cut onions in half crosswise to make 4 thick "wheels." Place in bottom of slow cooker.
2. Sear both sides of chops in hot olive oil in a heavy skillet, about 2 to 3 minutes on each side. Place in cooker on top of onions. Sprinkle with pepper.
3. Dissolve bouillon cubes in boiling water. Stir in mustard. Pour into slow cooker.
4. Cover and cook on high 3 hours or until pork and onions are tender.

With two slow cookers, you can prepare **Perfect Pork Chops** and **Chunk-Style Applesauce** at the same time. If you have only one cooker, make the applesauce the day before and chill it; it's mouthwatering warm or cold. Plus, you'll be glad there's enough applesauce to serve another day.

editor's favorite
Chunk-Style Applesauce

makes 8 servings
ideal slow cooker: 3- or 3½-quart

8 large cooking apples, peeled,
   cored, and cut into chunks
½ cup water
1 tsp. ground cinnamon
½ cup sugar

1. Combine all ingredients in slow cooker.
2. Cover and cook on high 3 to 4 hours or on low 8 hours.
3. Serve warm. (This sauce is also delicious served chilled.)

Buttered Green Beans

makes 4 to 6 servings

1½ lbs. fresh green beans
¾ cup water
¼ cup butter or margarine
Salt and pepper to taste

1. Trim ends from green beans and remove strings.
2. Bring water to a boil in a large saucepan; add beans. Cover, reduce heat, and simmer 10 to 12 minutes or until crisp-tender, stirring occasionally. Drain beans; add butter, salt, and pepper. Toss until butter melts.

entertaining
Fudge Pie

makes 1 (9-inch) pie

¾ cup butter or margarine
3 1-oz. unsweetened chocolate
   baking squares
3 eggs
1½ cups sugar
¾ cup all-purpose flour
1 tsp. vanilla extract
¾ cup chopped pecans, toasted
   and divided
Toppings: vanilla ice cream,
   chocolate syrup

1. Cook butter and chocolate in a small saucepan over low heat, stirring often until melted.
2. Beat eggs at medium speed with an electric mixer 5 minutes. Gradually add sugar, beating until blended. Gradually add chocolate mixture, flour, and vanilla, beating until blended. Stir in ½ cup pecans.
3. Pour mixture into a lightly greased 9-inch pieplate.
4. Bake at 350° for 35 to 40 minutes or until center is firm. Cool. Top each serving with vanilla ice cream and chocolate syrup; sprinkle with remaining chopped pecans.

chic chicken dinner

serves 4

Baked Chicken Breasts

Lemon Couscous   Spinach-Apple Salad

Tiny Cream Cheese Biscuits

**Baked Chicken Breasts,
Lemon Couscous, Spinach-Apple Salad,
Tiny Cream Cheese Biscuits**

Baked Chicken Breasts

makes 4 servings
ideal slow cooker: 4-quart

4 bone-in chicken breast halves,
  skinned
2 Tbsp. butter or margarine
10¾-oz. can cream of chicken soup
½ cup dry sherry
1 tsp. dried tarragon or rosemary,
  or both
1 tsp. Worcestershire sauce
¼ tsp. garlic powder
8-oz. container sliced fresh
  mushrooms

1. Place chicken breasts in slow
cooker.
2. In a saucepan, combine remaining
ingredients. Heat until smooth
and hot. Pour over chicken.
3. Cover and cook on low 4½
hours.

Lemon Couscous

makes 4 servings

1½ cups chicken broth
1 Tbsp. grated lemon rind
3 Tbsp. fresh lemon juice
1 Tbsp. butter or margarine
¼ tsp. salt
1 cup couscous, uncooked
3 Tbsp. pecan pieces, toasted
3 Tbsp. chopped fresh parsley
2-oz. jar sliced pimiento, drained

1. Combine first 5 ingredients in
a saucepan; bring to a boil. Add
couscous, stirring well; cover,
remove from heat, and let stand
5 minutes. Fluff couscous with a
fork. Stir in pecans, parsley, and
pimiento.

Dress up an ordinary chicken dinner with this casually
chic menu. A little sherry really refines the flavor of
Baked Chicken Breasts from your slow cooker. The
couscous, spinach salad, and petite biscuit bites are
extra-quick to make on the side.

Spinach-Apple Salad

makes 4 servings

4 bacon slices
4 cups tightly packed fresh baby
  spinach (½ lb.)
1 large Red Delicious apple,
  unpeeled, cored, and thinly
  sliced
⅓ cup mayonnaise
¼ cup frozen orange juice
  concentrate, thawed and
  undiluted
Freshly ground pepper

1. Place bacon on a microwave-safe
rack in a baking dish; cover with
paper towels. Microwave at HIGH
3 to 4 minutes or until crisp.
Crumble bacon and set aside.
2. Combine spinach, apple, and
bacon in a large bowl. Combine
mayonnaise and orange juice concentrate. Add to spinach mixture;
toss gently. Sprinkle with pepper.

Tiny Cream Cheese Biscuits

makes 1½ dozen

8-oz. pkg. cream cheese, softened
½ cup butter or margarine,
  softened
1 cup self-rising flour

1. Beat cream cheese and butter
at medium speed with an electric
mixer 2 minutes or until creamy.
Gradually add flour, beating at low
speed just until blended.
2. Spoon dough into ungreased
miniature (1¾-inch) muffin pans,
filling full. Bake at 400° for 15 to
17 minutes or until golden. Serve
biscuits hot.

ladies' luncheon

serves 6

Autumn Chicken Salad

Cucumber Sandwiches   Hot Fruit Punch

Lemon Poppy Seed Upside-Down Cake

**Lemon Poppy Seed
Upside-Down Cake**

make-ahead
Autumn Chicken Salad

makes 6 servings

Dried cranberries are sweeter than you might expect. Honey mustard dressing adds the perfect contrast to complement the sweetness.

3 cups chopped cooked chicken
¾ cup dried cranberries
3 celery ribs, chopped
1 medium-sized Red Delicious apple, chopped
½ cup pecan halves, toasted
¾ cup honey mustard dressing (we used Maple Grove Farms of Vermont)
Green leaf lettuce leaves

1. Stir together first 6 ingredients in a large bowl. Cover and chill. Serve on lettuce leaves.

make-ahead
Cucumber Sandwiches

makes 16 sandwiches

1 large cucumber, peeled, seeded, and grated
8-oz. pkg. cream cheese, softened
1 Tbsp. mayonnaise
1 small shallot, minced
¼ tsp. seasoned salt
16-oz. loaf sliced sandwich bread, crusts removed

1. Drain cucumber well, pressing between layers of paper towels.

Luscious **Lemon Poppy Seed Upside-Down Cake** is the star of this luncheon menu. Prepare it at least two hours ahead, and then slow cook **Hot Fruit Punch** in the same cooker an hour before guests arrive. Make **Autumn Chicken Salad** and **Cucumber Sandwiches** ahead at your leisure.

2. Stir together cucumber, cream cheese, and next 3 ingredients. Spread mixture over half of bread slices, and top with remaining bread slices.
3. Cut sandwiches in half diagonally. Store in an airtight container in refrigerator.

15-minute prep
Hot Fruit Punch

makes 10 1-cup servings
ideal slow cooker: 4- or 5-quart

1 qt. cranberry juice
3 cups water
6-oz. can frozen orange juice concentrate, thawed
10-oz. pkg. frozen red raspberries, thawed
2 oranges, sliced
6 cinnamon sticks
12 whole allspice

1. Combine all ingredients in slow cooker.
2. Cover and cook on high 1 hour or until hot. Remove spices. Turn to low while serving.

editor's favorite • make-ahead
Lemon Poppy Seed Upside-Down Cake

makes 8 to 10 servings
ideal slow cooker: 3½- or 4-quart round

15.8-oz. pkg. lemon poppy seed bread mix (we used Betty Crocker; reserve glaze packet for another use)
1 egg
8 oz. container light sour cream
½ cup water
1 Tbsp. butter
¾ cup water
½ cup sugar
¼ cup lemon juice

1. Combine first 4 ingredients until well moistened. Spread in lightly greased slow cooker.
2. Combine butter and remaining 3 ingredients in a small saucepan. Bring to a boil. Pour boiling mixture over batter.
3. Cover and cook on high 2 to 2½ hours. Edges will be slightly brown. Turn off heat and leave in cooker for 30 minutes with cover slightly ajar.
4. When cool enough to handle, run a knife around edge of cake in cooker. Hold a large plate over top of cooker; invert, allowing sauce to drip over cake. Allow cake to cool before slicing.

down-home veggies

serves 6 to 8

Macaroni and Cheese

Simple Turnip Greens   A Mess o' Peas

Corn Bread from Scratch

Macaroni and Cheese, Simple Turnip Greens,
Corn Bread from Scratch, A Mess o' Peas

kid-friendly
Macaroni and Cheese

makes 6 to 8 servings
ideal slow cooker: 4-quart

8-oz. pkg. elbow macaroni, cooked
    al dente
13-oz. can evaporated milk
1 cup whole milk
¼ cup butter, melted
2 large eggs, slightly beaten
4 cups grated sharp cheddar
    cheese, divided
¼ to ½ tsp. salt to taste
⅛ tsp. white pepper
¼ cup grated Parmesan cheese

1. Combine lightly cooked
macaroni, evaporated milk, whole
milk, melted butter, eggs, 3 cups
cheddar cheese, salt, and pepper
in slow cooker.
2. Top with remaining 1 cup cheddar cheese and Parmesan cheese.
3. Cover and cook on low 3 hours.

5 ingredients or less
Simple Turnip Greens

makes 6 to 8 servings

1 bunch fresh turnip greens (about
    4½ lbs.)
1 lb. salt pork (streak of lean) or
    smoked pork shoulder
3 qts. water
¼ tsp. freshly ground pepper
2 tsp. sugar (optional)

1. Remove and discard stems and
discolored spots from greens.
Wash greens thoroughly; drain
and tear into pieces. Set aside.
2. Slice salt pork at ¼-inch intervals, cutting to, but not through,
the skin.

3. Combine salt pork, water,
pepper, and, if desired, sugar in a
Dutch oven; bring to a boil. Cover,
reduce heat, and simmer 1 hour.
4. Add greens and cook, uncovered, 30 to 35 minutes or until
tender. Serve with a slotted spoon.

note:

: • Sugar can be added during
cooking to eliminate a bitter
taste, although this technique is
sometimes debated.

A Mess o' Peas

makes 8 to 10 servings

1 qt. water
8- to 10-oz. smoked ham hock
8 cups fresh field peas
4 to 6 hot peppers in vinegar,
    drained
1 tsp. sugar
1 tsp. salt
1 tsp. black pepper

1. Bring water and smoked ham
hock to a boil in a large Dutch
oven over medium-high heat.
Reduce heat to low and simmer
30 minutes. Stir in peas and
remaining ingredients; cover and
simmer 25 to 30 minutes or until
peas are done.

You won't miss the meat in this classic, down-home
vegetable plate. If you're short on time, substitute
store-bought corn bread for **Corn Bread from Scratch.**

Corn Bread from Scratch

makes 9 servings
ideal slow cooker: 6-quart

1¼ cups all-purpose flour
¾ cup yellow cornmeal
¼ cup sugar
1 Tbsp. baking powder
½ tsp. salt
1 egg, slightly beaten
1 cup fat-free milk
¼ cup canola oil

1. In mixing bowl, sift together
flour, cornmeal, sugar, baking
powder, and salt. Make a well in
center.
2. Pour egg, milk, and oil into
well. Mix into dry mixture until
just moistened.
3. Pour mixture into a lightly
greased 1½-quart soufflé dish that
will fit into cooker. Cover dish
with aluminum foil. Place a trivet
or rack in slow cooker. Pour 1 cup
water in slow cooker and insert
soufflé dish.
4. Cover; cook on high 2 to 3
hours.

family favorites

serves 6 to 8

Turkey Meat Loaf

Homestyle Mashed Potatoes   peas and carrots

Strawberry Shortcake

Turkey Meat Loaf,
Homestyle Mashed Potatoes

Turkey Meat Loaf

makes 8 servings

ideal slow cooker: 3- or 4-quart oval

1½ lbs. lean ground turkey
2 eggs
⅓ cup ketchup
1 Tbsp. Worcestershire sauce
½ cup chopped fresh basil
1 tsp. salt
½ tsp. black pepper
1 small onion, finely chopped
1 medium baking potato, peeled
    and shredded (2 cups shredded
    potato)
½ cup finely chopped red bell
    pepper
½ cup seasoned bread crumbs
⅔ cup ketchup
1 Tbsp. Worcestershire sauce

1. Combine first 11 ingredients in a large bowl.
2. Shape into a loaf slightly smaller than slow cooker and place in cooker.
3. Cover and cook on high 1 hour and then on low 2½ to 3 more hours. Carefully drain off liquid.
4. Stir together ⅔ cup ketchup and 1 Tbsp. Worcestershire sauce. Spread glaze on top of loaf. Cover and cook on low 1 hour or until a meat thermometer registers 165°.
5. Allow loaf to cool about 15 minutes in slow cooker. Gently remove loaf from cooker using a large metal spatula.

Traditional meat loaf gets a quick and healthy face-lift with lean ground turkey meat and hands-off cooking in the slow cooker. Serve with **Homestyle Mashed Potatoes** and **Strawberry Shortcake** to complete this perfect family meal. It's sure to become a staple and a favorite.

Homestyle Mashed Potatoes

makes 6 to 8 servings

One of the keys to fluffy spuds is returning the cooked potatoes to the warm, dry pan you cooked them in for mashing.

2 lbs. medium potatoes, peeled
    and quartered (we tested with
    Yukon gold)
¼ cup butter or margarine
½ cup whipping cream
1 tsp. salt
½ tsp. freshly ground pepper

1. Cook potatoes in boiling water to cover 20 to 25 minutes or until very tender. Drain well and return potatoes to pan. Add butter and mash until butter melts, using a potato masher. Add cream, salt, and pepper; mash to desired texture.

note:

• Yukon gold potatoes are yellow-fleshed potatoes known for their buttery flavor and creamy texture. Quite versatile, they can be used for baking, broiling, or frying—but we particularly like them mashed.

Strawberry Shortcake

makes 8 servings

4 cups sliced fresh or frozen
    strawberries, thawed
½ cup sugar
2 cups biscuit and baking mix
⅔ cup half-and-half
¼ cup butter or margarine, melted
2 Tbsp. sugar
1 large egg, lightly beaten
1 Tbsp. sugar
8-oz. container frozen whipped
    topping, thawed

1. Combine strawberries and ½ cup sugar, stirring gently. Cover and chill at least 20 minutes.
2. Meanwhile, combine biscuit and baking mix and next 4 ingredients; beat at high speed of an electric mixer 30 seconds. Spoon batter into a greased 8-inch round cake pan; sprinkle with 1 Tbsp. sugar. Bake at 425° for 15 to 20 minutes or until golden. Let cool in pan on a wire rack 10 minutes; remove from pan and let cool completely on wire rack.
3. Split shortcake in half horizontally. Place bottom half, cut side up, on a serving plate. Spoon half each of strawberry mixture and whipped topping over shortcake. Top with remaining shortcake. Spoon remaining whipped topping and strawberry mixture on top.

dip 'n' sip

serves 6 to 8

Barbara Jean's Pizza Dip

Quick Creamy Vegetable Dip   Ginger Beer

Chocolate Fondue

Chocolate Fondue

Barbara Jean's Pizza Dip

makes 8 to 10 servings
ideal slow cooker: 2- or 3-quart

4 ozs. mozzarella cheese, shredded
4 ozs. Cheddar cheese, shredded
1 green bell pepper, minced
5-oz. can sliced black olives
5-oz. jar sliced stuffed green olives
4 ozs. sliced mushrooms
1 cup mayonnaise
Pepperoni slices, cut up

1. Combine all ingredients except pepperoni in slow cooker.
2. Top with pepperoni.
3. Cover and cook on low 2 hours.
4. Stir well before bringing to the buffet or table.
5. Serve with snack crackers or breadsticks.

make-ahead
Quick Creamy Vegetable Dip

makes 6 to 8 servings

½ cup mayonnaise
½ cup sour cream
2-oz. jar diced pimiento, drained
¼ cup chopped onion
¼ cup diced green bell pepper
½ tsp. garlic salt
⅛ tsp. black pepper
⅛ tsp. hot sauce

1. Stir together all ingredients. Cover and chill 2 hours.
2. Serve with cut vegetables.

Cook and serve both hot dips, **Barbara Jean's Pizza Dip** and **Chocolate Fondue,** in slow cookers (you'll need two) for this festive gathering. A chilled vegetable dip and a refreshing ginger-brewed beverage round out the menu and carry out the fun theme.

make-ahead
Ginger Beer

makes 10 1-cup servings

There's actually no beer involved here. Just a generous quantity of grated fresh ginger that "brews" for a time in a sugar syrup. This pungent refresher also tastes great hot. Just heat it in the microwave by the mugful.

2 qts. water
2 cups sugar
⅔ cup grated fresh ginger
1 Tbsp. grated lime rind
¼ cup fresh lime juice

1. Combine all ingredients, stirring until sugar dissolves. Cover and chill 4 hours.
2. Pour ginger mixture through a wire-mesh strainer into a large pitcher, and discard solids. Chill until ready to serve. Serve over crushed ice.

editor's favorite • entertaining
Chocolate Fondue

makes 6 to 8 servings
ideal slow cooker: 1½- or 2-quart

1 pkg. (8 squares) semisweet chocolate, coarsely chopped
4-oz. pkg. sweet baking chocolate, coarsely chopped
14-oz. can sweetened condensed milk
2 Tbsp. Kirsch or favorite flavored liqueur
Sponge cake squares, strawberries, kiwi slices, pineapple chunks

1. Place chocolates and milk in slow cooker. Cover. Stir occasionally until melted and smooth, about 1 hour.
2. Stir in Kirsch.
3. Bring fondue to table, along with sponge cake squares, strawberries, kiwi slices, and pineapple chunks to dip into it.

pot roast dinner

serves 6

Pot Roast with Gravy and Vegetables

Green Bean-Feta Salad   biscuits or rolls

Berry-Lemon Cream Pie

**Pot Roast with
Gravy and Vegetables**

Pot Roast with Gravy and Vegetables

makes 4 to 6 servings
ideal slow cooker: 6-quart

3- to 4-lb. bottom round, rump, or
    arm roast, cut in half
2 to 3 tsp. salt
½ tsp. black pepper
2 Tbsp. all-purpose flour
¼ cup cold water
1 tsp. kitchen bouquet or gravy
    browning seasoning sauce
1 garlic clove, minced
2 medium onions, cut into wedges
4 to 6 medium-sized red potatoes,
    halved
2 to 4 carrots, quartered
1 green bell pepper, sliced

1. Place roast in slow cooker.
Sprinkle with salt and pepper.
2. Make paste of flour and cold
water. Stir in kitchen bouquet and
pour over roast.
3. Add garlic, onions, potatoes,
carrots, and green peppers.
4. Cover and cook on high 4 to 5
hours or on high 1 hour and then
on low 6 to 8 hours.
5. Taste and adjust seasonings
before serving.

Green Bean-Feta Salad

makes 6 to 8 servings

1½ lbs. fresh green beans,
    trimmed
½ cup chopped red onion
½ cup Lemon Vinaigrette
½ cup crumbled feta cheese
½ cup walnuts, toasted and
    chopped

Pot Roast with Gravy and Vegetables slow cooks all day while you're away. Make and chill the salad and dessert a day ahead for the best flavor and taste. Dinner's ready as soon as you can reheat store-bought biscuits or rolls for sopping up the gravy.

1. Cook green beans in boiling
salted water to cover 8 minutes
or until crisp-tender. Drain and
plunge into ice water to stop the
cooking process; drain and pat
dry. Place in a serving bowl; cover
and chill at least 2 hours.
2. Add chopped onion and Lemon
Vinaigrette to beans, tossing
to coat. Sprinkle with feta and
walnuts.

lemon vinaigrette

makes about 1 cup

*Use leftover vinaigrette to marinate
artichoke hearts or chicken breasts, or
serve over salad niçoise.*

3 Tbsp. fresh lemon juice
3 Tbsp. white wine vinegar
1 Tbsp. Dijon mustard
½ tsp. sugar
¼ tsp. salt
⅛ tsp. freshly ground pepper
½ cup oil

1. Whisk together first 6 ingredients in a small bowl; gradually
whisk in oil until blended.

Berry-Lemon Cream Pie

makes 1 (9-inch) pie

1⅔ cups graham cracker crumbs
¼ cup granulated sugar
⅓ cup butter or margarine,
    melted
8-oz. pkg. cream cheese, softened
14-oz. can sweetened condensed
    milk
¼ cup powdered sugar
3.4-oz. pkg. lemon instant pudding
    mix
2 tsp. grated lemon rind
½ cup fresh lemon juice
1 pt. fresh blueberries
2 Tbsp. blueberry preserves
1 cup whipping cream

1. Stir together first 3 ingredients;
press in bottom and up sides of a
9-inch pieplate. Bake at 350° for
8 minutes; remove to a wire rack
and cool completely.
2. Beat cheese, milk, and powdered sugar with an electric mixer
until creamy. Add pudding mix,
rind, and juice; beat until blended.
Spread half of mixture into crust.
3. Stir together blueberries and
preserves; spread berries over
lemon mixture. Spread remaining
lemon mixture over blueberry
mixture; cover and chill until set.
4. Beat cream until soft peaks form
and spread over top of pie. Store in
refrigerator.

Green Bean Casserole
(page 50)

holiday gatherings

Baked Brie with Cranberry Chutney

makes 25 servings
ideal slow cooker: 1-quart

1 cup fresh or dried cranberries
½ cup brown sugar
⅓ cup cider vinegar
2 Tbsp. water or orange juice
2 tsp. minced crystallized ginger
¼ tsp. cinnamon
⅛ tsp. ground cloves
Vegetable oil
8-oz. round of Brie cheese
1 Tbsp. sliced almonds, toasted

1. Mix together cranberries, brown sugar, vinegar, water, ginger, cinnamon, and cloves in slow cooker.
2. Cover and cook on low 4 hours. Stir once near the end to see if it is thickening. If not, remove top, turn slow cooker to high, and cook 30 minutes without lid.
3. Put cranberry chutney in covered container and chill for up to 2 weeks. When ready to serve, bring to room temperature.

4. Brush ovenproof plate with oil, place unpeeled Brie on plate, and bake uncovered at 350° for 9 minutes, until cheese is soft and partially melted. Remove from oven.
5. Top with half the chutney and garnish with toasted almonds. Serve with crackers.

5 ingredients or less
Cranberry Franks

makes 15 to 20 servings
ideal slow cooker: 4- or 5-quart

Great picnic, potluck, or buffet food.

2 pkgs. cocktail wieners or little smoked sausages
16-oz. can jellied cranberry sauce
1 cup ketchup
3 Tbsp. brown sugar
1 Tbsp. lemon juice

1. Combine all ingredients in slow cooker.
2. Cover and cook on high 1 to 2 hours.

editor's favorite
Holiday Meatballs

makes 20 servings
ideal slow cooker: 6-quart

2 15-oz. bottles hot ketchup
2 cups blackberry wine
2 12-oz. jars apple jelly
2 lbs. frozen precooked meatballs, thawed, or your own favorite meatballs, cooked

1. Combine ketchup, wine, and jelly in slow cooker. Cover and cook on high 1 hour or until heated.
2. Add meatballs.
3. Cover and cook on high 3 to 4 hours.

variations:

• For those who like meatballs hot and spicy, put a bottle of XXXtra hot sauce on the table for them to add to their individual servings.
• If you prefer a less winey flavor, use 1 cup water and only 1 cup wine.

Spicy Autumn Punch

makes 16 servings
ideal slow cooker: 4-quart

8 whole cloves
2 oranges
6 cups apple juice
1 cinnamon stick
¼ tsp. ground nutmeg
3 Tbsp. lemon juice
¼ cup honey
2¼ cups pineapple juice

1. Press cloves into oranges. Bake at 325° to 350° for 30 minutes.
2. Meanwhile, combine apple juice and cinnamon stick in slow cooker.
3. Cover and cook on high 1 hour.
4. Add remaining ingredients except oranges.
5. Cover and cook on low 2 to 3 hours. Add oranges at end, either whole or in quarters.

Carolers' Hot Chocolate

makes 13 1-cup servings
ideal slow cooker: 4½- or 5-quart

10 cups milk
¾ cup sugar
¾ cup unsweetened cocoa powder
   or hot chocolate mix
½ tsp. salt
2 cups hot water
Marshmallows (optional)

1. Pour milk into slow cooker. Turn on high.
2. Stir together sugar, cocoa, and salt in a heavy pan. Add hot water. Stir and boil 3 minutes, stirring often.
3. Stir into slow cooker. Cover and cook on high 2 to 2½ hours. Serve with marshmallows, if desired.

Mocha Eggnog

makes 8 servings
ideal slow cooker: 2-quart

1 qt. low-fat eggnog
1 Tbsp. instant decaf French vanilla
   coffee granules
¼ cup coffee-flavored liqueur

1. Combine eggnog and coffee granules in slow cooker.
2. Cover and cook until mixture is hot and coffee granules dissolve.
3. Add coffee liqueur just before serving.
4. Ladle into mugs.

note:

• If you like, serve the eggnog topped with a spoonful of low-fat whipping cream and a sprinkling of shaved chocolate.

15-minute prep
Holiday Wassail

makes 8 1-cup servings
ideal slow cooker: 3- or 4-quart

16-oz. can apricot halves,
   undrained
18 whole cloves
6 3½-inch cinnamon sticks, broken
4 cups unsweetened pineapple
   juice
2 cups apple cider
1 cup orange juice

1. In a blender or food processor, blend apricots with their juice until smooth.
2. Place cloves and cinnamon sticks in a cheesecloth bag.
3. Place all ingredients in slow cooker. Cover and cook on low 3 to 4 hours. Serve hot.

editor's favorite
Maple Mulled Cider

makes 8 1-cup servings
ideal slow cooker: 3- or 4-quart

½ gal. cider
3 to 4 cinnamon sticks
2 tsp. whole cloves
2 tsp. whole allspice
1 to 2 Tbsp. orange juice
   concentrate (optional)
1 to 2 Tbsp. maple syrup
Cinnamon sticks (optional)

1. Combine first 6 ingredients in slow cooker.
2. Cover and cook on low 2 hours. Strain solids and discard.
3. Garnish filled glasses with cinnamon sticks, if desired.

Cider Snap

makes 12 to 16 servings
ideal slow cooker: 4-quart

2 qts. apple cider or apple juice
4 Tbsp. hot cinnamon candies
At least 16 apple slices
At least 16 cinnamon sticks

1. Combine cider and cinnamon candies in slow cooker.
2. Cover and cook on high 2 hours until candies dissolve and cider is hot.
3. Ladle into mugs and serve with apple-slice floaters and cinnamon-stick stirrers.

note:

• This is a cold-winter-night luxury. Make the cider in the morning and keep it on low throughout the day so its fragrance fills the house.

Maple Mulled Cider

smooth in small bowl. Stir into beef broth. Bring to a boil. Cook and stir 2 minutes until thickened.
8. Slice pot roast and serve with gravy.

Ham with Sweet Potatoes and Oranges

makes 4 servings
ideal slow cooker: 4-quart oval

2 to 3 sweet potatoes, peeled and sliced ¼-inch thick
1 large cooked ham slice
3 seedless oranges, peeled and sliced crosswise
3 Tbsp. orange juice concentrate
3 Tbsp. honey
½ cup brown sugar
2 Tbsp. cornstarch

1. Place sweet potatoes in slow cooker.
2. Arrange ham and orange slices on top.
3. Combine remaining ingredients. Drizzle over ham and oranges.
4. Cover and cook on low 7 to 8 hours.
5. Serve with lime gelatin salad.

Apple-and-Onion Beef Pot Roast

makes 8 to 10 servings
ideal slow cooker: 4- or 5-quart

3-lb. boneless beef roast, cut in half
Oil
1 cup water
1 tsp. seasoning salt
½ tsp. soy sauce
½ tsp. Worcestershire sauce
¼ tsp. garlic powder
1 large tart apple, quartered
1 large onion, sliced
2 Tbsp. cornstarch
2 Tbsp. water

1. Brown roast on all sides in oil in skillet. Place in slow cooker.
2. Add 1 cup water to skillet to loosen browned bits. Pour over roast.
3. Sprinkle with seasoning salt, soy sauce, Worcestershire sauce, and garlic powder.
4. Top with apple and onion.
5. Cover and cook on low 5 to 6 hours.
6. Remove roast and onion. Discard apple. Let stand 15 minutes.
7. To make gravy, pour juices from roast into saucepan and simmer until reduced to 2 cups. Combine cornstarch and 2 Tbsp. water until

editor's favorite

Cottage Cheese Bread

makes 8 servings
ideal slow cooker: 3-quart

1 cup cottage cheese
2 eggs
1 cup sugar
¾ cup 2% milk
1 tsp. vanilla extract
2¾ cups buttermilk baking mix

2 tsp. orange zest
Garnish: orange zest (optional)

1. Combine all ingredients in a mixing bowl.
2. Pour into greased slow cooker.
3. Cover and cook on high 1 hour.

give insert a half turn and replace in cooking unit.
4. Cook on high 45 minutes to 1 hour longer.
5. Uncover and let stand 15 minutes. Turn out onto a plate to serve.
6. Garnish with orange zest, if

Orange Chicken with Sweet Potatoes

makes 6 servings
ideal slow cooker: 5-quart

2 or 3 sweet potatoes, peeled and
   sliced
6 boneless, skinless chicken breast
   halves
⅔ cup all-purpose flour
1 tsp. salt
1 tsp. ground nutmeg
½ tsp. ground cinnamon
Dash of pepper
Dash of garlic powder
10¾-oz. can cream of celery or
   cream of chicken soup
4-oz. can sliced mushrooms,
   drained
½ cup orange juice
½ tsp. grated orange rind
2 tsp. brown sugar
3 Tbsp. all-purpose flour

1. Place sweet potatoes in slow
cooker.
2. Rinse chicken and pat dry.
Combine flour, salt, nutmeg,
cinnamon, pepper, and garlic
powder. Thoroughly coat chicken
in flour mixture. Place on top of
sweet potatoes.
3. Combine soup and remaining
ingredients. Stir well. Pour over
chicken.
4. Cover and cook on high 3 to 4
hours or on low 8 to 10 hours.
5. Serve over rice.

5 ingredients or less
Chicken and Dumplings

makes 5 to 6 servings
ideal slow cooker: 3- or 4-quart

1 lb. boneless, skinless chicken
   breast halves, cut in 1-inch
   cubes
1 lb. frozen vegetables of your
   choice
1 medium onion, diced
2 12-oz. jars fat-free, low-sodium
   chicken broth, divided
1½ cups low-fat buttermilk
   biscuit mix

1. Combine chicken, frozen
vegetables, onion, and chicken
broth (reserve ½ cup plus 1 Tbsp.
broth) in slow cooker.
2. Cover and cook on high 2
hours.
3. Combine biscuit mix and
reserved broth until moistened.
Drop by tablespoonfuls over hot
chicken and vegetables.
4. Cover and cook on high 10
minutes.
5. Uncover and cook on high 20
minutes more.

Saucy Turkey Breast

makes 6 servings
ideal slow cooker: 5- or 6-quart

3-lb. boneless turkey breast
16-oz. can whole-berry cranberry
   sauce
1-oz. envelope dry onion soup mix
½ cup orange juice
¼ tsp. freshly ground pepper

1. Place turkey breast in slow
cooker; reserve gravy packet for
another use.

2. Combine cranberry sauce and
remaining 3 ingredients in a
medium bowl, stirring well. Pour
cranberry mixture over turkey.
3. Cover and cook on high 2½
hours. Remove turkey to a serving platter; cover and let stand
10 minutes before slicing. Spoon
about ½ cup sauce over turkey
slices; serve with remaining sauce.

Turkey Breast with Orange Sauce

makes 4 to 6 servings
ideal slow cooker: 4- or 5-quart

*This very easy, impressive-looking
and -tasting recipe is perfect for
company.*

1 large onion, chopped
3 garlic cloves, minced
1 tsp. dried rosemary
½ tsp. pepper
2- to 3-lb. boneless, skinless turkey
   breast
1½ cups orange juice

1. Place onion in slow cooker.
2. Combine garlic, rosemary, and
pepper in a bowl.
3. Make gashes in turkey, about
three-fourths of the way through
at 2-inch intervals. Stuff with
herb mixture. Place turkey in slow
cooker.
4. Pour juice over turkey.
5. Cover and cook on high 1 hour
and then on low 5 to 6 hours or
until turkey is no longer pink in
center.

Brussels Sprouts with Pimientos

makes 8 servings
ideal slow cooker: 3½- or 4-quart

2 lbs. fresh Brussels sprouts
¼ tsp. dried oregano
½ tsp. dried basil
2-oz. jar pimientos, drained
¼ cup or 2.25-oz. can sliced black
    olives, drained
1 Tbsp. olive oil
½ cup water

1. Combine all ingredients in slow cooker.
2. Cover and cook on low 6 hours.

Cranberry-Orange Beets

makes 6 servings
ideal slow cooker: 6-quart

2 lbs. medium beets, peeled and
    quartered
½ tsp. ground nutmeg
1 cup cranberry juice
1 tsp. orange peel, finely shredded
    (optional)
2 Tbsp. butter
2 Tbsp. sugar
4 tsp. cornstarch

1. Place beets in slow cooker. Sprinkle with nutmeg.
2. Add cranberry juice and, if desired, orange peel. Dot with butter.
3. Cover and cook on high 3 to 3½ hours or on low 6 to 7 hours.
4. In small bowl, combine sugar and cornstarch.
5. Remove ½ cup cooking liquid and stir into cornstarch mixture.
6. Stir into slow cooker.
7. Cover and cook on high 15 to 30 minutes.

Super Creamed Corn

makes 8 to 12 servings
ideal slow cooker: 4-quart

This side dish is a welcome addition to a holiday menu. It's easy and requires no last-minute preparation.

2 to 3 lbs. frozen whole-kernel
    corn
8-oz. pkg. cream cheese, cubed
¼ cup butter or margarine, melted
2 to 3 Tbsp. sugar or honey
2 to 3 Tbsp. water (optional)

1. Combine all ingredients in slow cooker.
2. Cover and cook on low 4 hours.
3. Serve with meat loaf, turkey, or hamburgers.

Green Bean Casserole

makes 6 servings
ideal slow cooker: 4-quart

pictured on page 44

This slow-cooked version of the holiday classic is better than the original because it frees up your oven for other holiday treats.

2 lbs. fresh green beans, halved,
    or 4 10-oz. pkgs. frozen green
    beans
10¾-oz. can cream of mushroom
    soup
3-oz. can French fried onion rings
1 cup grated Cheddar cheese
8-oz. can water chestnuts, thinly
    sliced
Slivered almonds (optional)
Salt to taste
Pepper to taste
1 cup water

1. In slow cooker, layer one-third of ingredients, except water, in order given. Repeat 2 times, saving a few onion rings for top.
2. Pour water into slow cooker.
3. Cover and cook on high 4 to 5 hours or on low 8 to 10 hours. Sprinkle reserved onion rings on top 20 minutes before serving.

Orange-Glazed Carrots

makes 6 to 8 servings
ideal slow cooker: 3½-quart

32-oz. pkg. baby carrots
¼ cup firmly packed brown sugar
½ cup orange juice
1 Tbsp. butter
½ to ¾ tsp. ground cinnamon,
    according to your taste
    preference
¼ tsp. ground nutmeg
2 Tbsp. cornstarch
¼ cup water

1. Combine all ingredients except cornstarch and water in slow cooker.
2. Cover and cook on low 4 to 6 hours or until carrots are done to your liking.
3. Put carrots in serving dish and keep warm, reserving cooking juices. Put reserved juices in small saucepan. Bring to boil.
4. Mix cornstarch and water in small bowl until blended. Add to juices. Boil 1 minute or until thickened, stirring constantly.
5. Pour over carrots and serve.

Caramelized Pears
in Wine

Caramelized Pears in Wine

makes 6 servings
ideal slow cooker: 5-quart oval

6 medium-sized fresh pears with
    stems
1 cup sweet white wine (Sauternes
    works well) or apple juice
½ cup sugar
½ cup water
3 Tbsp. lemon juice
2 cinnamon sticks, each about
    2½ to 3 inches long
3 whole cloves
¼ tsp. ground nutmeg
6 Tbsp. fat-free caramel apple dip

1. Peel pears, leaving whole with
stems intact.
2. Place pears upright in slow
cooker. Shave bottoms if needed
to level fruit.
3. Combine wine, sugar, water,
lemon juice, cinnamon, cloves,
and nutmeg. Pour wine mixture
over pears.
4. Cover and cook on low 4 to 6
hours or until pears are tender.
5. Cool pears in liquid.
6. Remove cinnamon sticks and
cloves from liquid. Transfer pears
to individual serving dishes. Place
2 tsp. cooking liquid in bottom of
each dish.
7. Microwave caramel dip according to package directions until
heated through, stirring every 20
seconds.
8. Drizzle caramel dip over pears
and serve immediately.

Sweet Potatoes and Apples

makes 8 servings
ideal slow cooker: 4-quart

3 large sweet potatoes, peeled
    and cubed
3 large tart and firm apples,
    peeled and sliced
½ tsp. salt
⅛ to ¼ tsp. pepper
1 tsp. ground sage
1 tsp. ground cinnamon
4 Tbsp. light, soft tub margarine,
    melted
2 Tbsp. maple syrup
Brown sugar substitute to equal
    1 Tbsp.
Toasted sliced almonds or chopped
    pecans (optional)

1. Place half the sweet potatoes in
slow cooker. Layer half the apple
slices on top of sweet potatoes.
2. Stir together dry seasonings.
Sprinkle half over apples.
3. Stir together margarine, maple
syrup, and sugar substitute. Spoon
half over seasonings.
4. Repeat layers.
5. Cover and cook on low 6 to 8
hours or until potatoes are soft,
stirring occasionally.
6. To add a bit of crunch, sprinkle
with toasted almonds or pecans
before serving.
7. Serve with pork or poultry.

Wanda's Chicken and
Rice Casserole (page 55)

15 minutes to prep

Tangy Cocktail Franks

makes 12 servings
ideal slow cooker: 3-quart

14-oz. jar currant jelly
¼ cup prepared mustard
3 Tbsp. dry sherry
¼ tsp. ground allspice
30-oz. can unsweetened pineapple
   chunks
6-oz. pkg. low-sodium cocktail
   franks

1. Melt jelly in slow cooker turned
on high. Stir in mustard, sherry,
and allspice until blended.
2. Drain pineapple chunks and
any liquid in cocktail franks
package. Discard juice. Gently stir
pineapple and franks into slow
cooker.
3. Cover and cook on low 1 to
2 hours.

Cheesy Hot Bean Dip

makes 4 to 5 cups
ideal slow cooker: 3-quart

16-oz. can refried beans
1 cup salsa
2 cups shredded Jack and Cheddar
   cheeses, mixed
1 cup sour cream
3-oz. pkg. cream cheese, cubed
1 Tbsp. chili powder
¼ tsp. ground cumin

1. Combine all ingredients in slow
cooker.
2. Cover and cook on high 2
hours. Stir 2 or 3 times during
cooking.
3. Serve warm with chips.

Can-It-Really-Be-So-Easy Roast Beef

makes 8 servings
ideal slow cooker: 4- or 5-quart

4-lb. beef roast, cut in half
10¾-oz. can cream of mushroom
   soup
2.8-oz. envelope dry onion soup
   mix
1 cup water

1. Place beef on double layer of
aluminum foil.
2. Combine soup and dry soup
mix. Spread on all sides of beef.
Wrap foil around beef. Place in
slow cooker. Pour water around
roast.
3. Cover and cook on high 1 hour
and then on low 4 to 6 hours or
until meat is tender.

Chili Casserole

makes 6 servings
ideal slow cooker: 4-quart

1 lb. bulk pork sausage
2 cups water
15½-oz. can chili beans
14½-oz. can diced tomatoes
¾ cup brown rice
¼ cup chopped onion
1 Tbsp. chili powder
1 tsp. Worcestershire sauce
1 tsp. prepared mustard
¾ tsp. salt
⅛ tsp. garlic powder
1 cup shredded Cheddar cheese

1. Combine all ingredients except cheese in slow cooker.
2. Cover and cook on high 1 hour and then on low 5 hours.
3. Stir in cheese during last 10 minutes of cooking.

Lamb Chops

makes 6 to 8 servings
ideal slow cooker: 4- or 5-quart

1 medium onion, sliced
1 tsp. dried oregano
½ tsp. dried thyme
½ tsp. garlic powder
¼ tsp. salt
⅛ tsp. pepper
6 to 8 loin lamb chops (1¾ to 2 lbs.)
2 garlic cloves, minced
¼ cup water

1. Place onion in slow cooker.
2. Combine oregano, thyme, garlic powder, salt, and pepper. Rub over lamb chops. Place in slow cooker. Top with garlic. Pour water down along side of cooker.

3. Cover and cook on high 1 hour and then on low 2 to 4 hours.

Cherry Pork Chops

makes 6 servings
ideal slow cooker: 4-quart

6 pork chops, each cut ¾-inch thick
1 Tbsp. vegetable oil
Salt to taste
Pepper to taste
1 cup cherry pie filling
2 tsp. lemon juice
½ tsp. instant chicken bouillon granules
⅛ tsp. ground mace

1. Brown pork chops in oil in skillet. Sprinkle each chop with salt and pepper.
2. Combine remaining ingredients in slow cooker. Mix well.
3. Place browned pork chops on top of cherry mixture.
4. Cover and cook on low 4 to 5 hours.
5. Place chops on platter. Spoon some of cherry sauce on top. Serve with remaining sauce and rice or baked potatoes

Ham and Hash Browns

makes 6 to 8 servings
ideal slow cooker: 4- or 5-quart

32-oz. pkg. frozen hash brown potatoes, thawed
2½ cups cubed cooked ham
2-oz. jar diced pimientos, drained
10¾-oz. can Cheddar cheese soup
¾ cup half-and-half or milk
Dash of pepper
Salt to taste

1. Combine potatoes, ham, and pimientos in slow cooker.
2. Combine soup, half-and-half, and seasonings. Pour over potatoes.
3. Cover and cook on low 6 to 8 hours.

variation:

⋮ • Add 4-oz. can mushrooms, drained, or ¼ lb. sliced fresh mushrooms to Step 1.

Bandito Chili Dogs

makes 10 servings
ideal slow cooker: 4-quart

This is a fun recipe to serve after a football game or outside activity. The main part of your meal is ready when you get home.

1 lb. hot dogs
2 15-oz. cans chili, with or without beans
10¾-oz. can condensed Cheddar cheese soup
4-oz. can chopped green chiles
10 hot dog buns
1 medium onion, chopped
1 to 2 cups corn chips, coarsely crushed
1 cup shredded Cheddar cheese

1. Place hot dogs in slow cooker.
2. Combine chili, soup, and green chiles. Pour over hot dogs.
3. Cover and cook on low heat 3 to 3½ hours.
4. Serve hot dogs in buns. Top with chili mixture, onion, corn chips, and cheese.

Chicken Cacciatore with Spaghetti

makes 4 to 5 servings
ideal slow cooker: 5- or 6-quart

2 onions, sliced
2½ to 3 lbs. chicken legs
2 garlic cloves, minced
14½-oz. can stewed tomatoes
8-oz. can tomato sauce
1 tsp. salt
¼ tsp. pepper
1 to 2 tsp. dried oregano
½ tsp. dried basil
1 bay leaf
¼ cup white wine

1. Place onion in slow cooker.
2. Lay chicken legs over onion.
3. Combine remaining ingredients. Pour over chicken.
4. Cover and cook on high 1 hour and then on low 4 to 4½ hours.
5. Remove bay leaf. Serve chicken over hot buttered spaghetti, linguini, or fettuccine.

Chicken Cacciatore with Spaghetti

Wanda's Chicken and Rice Casserole

makes 6 servings
ideal slow cooker: 5-quart

pictured on page 52

1 cup long grain rice, uncooked
3 cups water
2 tsp. low-sodium chicken bouillon granules
10¾-oz. can fat-free, low-sodium cream of chicken soup
2 cups chopped cooked chicken breasts
¼ tsp. garlic powder
1 tsp. onion salt
1 cup grated Cheddar cheese
16-oz. bag frozen broccoli, thawed

1. Combine all ingredients except broccoli in slow cooker.
2. Cover and cook on high 3 to 4 hours or on low 6 to 7 hours, stirring in broccoli 1 hour before end of cooking time.

note:

• If the casserole is too runny as the end of the cooking time nears, remove lid from slow cooker for 15 minutes while continuing to cook.

Teriyaki Chicken

makes 6 servings
ideal slow cooker: 4-quart

6 to 8 skinless chicken thighs
½ cup soy sauce
2 Tbsp. brown sugar
2 Tbsp. grated fresh ginger
2 garlic cloves, minced

1. Wash and dry chicken. Place in slow cooker.
2. Combine remaining ingredients. Pour over chicken.
3. Cover and cook on high 1 hour and then on low 6 to 7 hours.

Chicken Azteca

makes 10 to 12 servings
ideal slow cooker: 4- to 5-quart

2 15-oz. cans black beans, drained
4 cups frozen corn kernels, thawed
2 garlic cloves, minced
¾ tsp. ground cumin
2 cups chunky salsa, divided
10 boneless, skinless chicken breast
    halves
2 8-oz. pkgs. cream cheese, cubed
Cooked rice
Shredded Cheddar cheese

1. Combine beans, corn, garlic, cumin, and 1 cup salsa in slow cooker.
2. Arrange chicken breasts over top. Pour remaining 1 cup salsa over top.
3. Cover and cook on high 2 to 3 hours or on high 1 hour and then on low 2 to 4 hours.
4. Remove chicken and cut in bite-size pieces. Return to cooker.
5. Stir in cream cheese. Cover and cook on high until cream cheese melts.
6. Spoon chicken and sauce over cooked rice. Top with shredded cheese.

Fruited Wild Rice with Pecans

makes 4 servings
ideal slow cooker: 3-quart

½ cup chopped onion
2 Tbsp. margarine
6-oz. pkg. long grain and wild rice
Seasoning packet from wild rice pkg.
1½ cups hot water
⅔ cup apple juice
1 large tart apple, chopped
¼ cup raisins
¼ cup coarsely chopped pecans

1. Combine all ingredients except pecans in greased slow cooker.
2. Cover and cook on high 2 to 2½ hours.
3. Stir in pecans. Serve.

Broccoli Turkey Supreme

makes 8 servings
ideal slow cooker: 5- or 6-quart

4 cups cubed cooked turkey breast
10¾-oz. can cream of chicken soup
10-oz. pkg. frozen broccoli florets,
    thawed and drained
6.9-oz. pkg. low-sodium plain rice
    mix
1½ cups fat-free milk
1 cup fat-free chicken broth
1 cup chopped celery
8-oz. can sliced water chestnuts,
    drained
¾ cup low-fat mayonnaise
½ cup chopped onion

1. Combine all ingredients in slow cooker.
2. Cook, uncovered, on high 2 to 2½ hours or until rice is tender.

editor's favorite

Homestyle Chicken Noodle Soup

makes 6 to 8 servings
ideal slow cooker: 5-quart

3 32-oz. cans chicken broth
2 cups chopped cooked chicken
⅓ cup thinly sliced celery, lightly
    precooked in microwave
⅓ cup shredded or chopped carrots
4 cups "homestyle" noodles (wide
    egg noodles), uncooked

1. Combine all ingredients except noodles in slow cooker.
2. Cover and cook on low 4 to 5 hours. Add noodles; cook 15 minutes or until noodles are done.

kid-friendly

Cream Cheese-Potato Soup

makes 6 servings
ideal slow cooker: 3½-quart

3 cups water
1 cup diced cooked ham
5 medium potatoes, diced fine
8-oz. pkg. fat-free cream cheese,
    cubed
Half an onion, chopped
1 tsp. garlic salt
½ tsp. pepper
½ tsp. dried dill weed

1. Combine all ingredients in slow cooker.
2. Cover and cook on high 4 hours, stirring occasionally.
3. Turn to low until ready to serve.

Homestyle Chicken
Noodle Soup

editor's favorite

Chicken Tortilla Soup

makes 8 servings
ideal slow cooker: 4- or 5-quart

4 boneless, skinless chicken breast
   halves

2 15-oz. cans black beans,
   undrained

2 15-oz. cans low-sodium Mexican
   stewed tomatoes or Rotel
   tomatoes

1 cup low-sodium salsa (mild,
   medium, or hot)

4-oz. can chopped green chiles,
   undrained

14½-oz. can low-sodium tomato
   sauce

Baked tortilla chips

2 cups shredded fat-free Monterey
   Jack or Cheddar cheese

1. Combine all ingredients except
chips and cheese in slow cooker.

2. Cover and cook on high 1 hour
and then on low 6 hours.

3. Just before serving, remove
chicken breasts and cut in bite-
size pieces. Stir into soup.

4. To serve, put a handful of chips
in each individual soup bowl.
Ladle soup over chips. Top with
cheese.

Cream of Broccoli Soup

makes 6 to 8 servings
ideal slow cooker: 3½- or 4-quart

1 small onion, chopped
1 Tbsp. vegetable oil
20-oz. pkg. frozen broccoli,
   thawed
2 10¾-oz. cans fat-free,
   low-sodium cream of celery
   soup
10¾-oz. can fat-free, low-sodium
   cream of mushroom soup
1 cup shredded low-fat American
   cheese
2 soup cans fat-free milk

1. Sauté onion in oil in skillet until
soft. Drain. Place onion in slow
cooker.
2. Combine all ingredients in slow
cooker.
3. Cover and cook on low 3 to 4
hours.

kid-friendly
Santa Fe Chicken Soup

makes 6 to 8 servings
ideal slow cooker: 4- to 5-quart

4 skinless, boneless chicken breast
   halves, cooked and shredded
1 small onion, diced
15¼-oz. can whole-kernel corn,
   undrained
24-oz. can pinto beans, undrained
14½-oz. can diced tomatoes,
   undrained
10-oz. can Rotel tomatoes,
   undrained
½ lb. mild Velveeta cheese, cubed
½ lb. regular Velveeta cheese,
   cubed
¼ cup milk

1. Place chicken and onion in slow
cooker.
2. Add remaining ingredients.
3. Cover and cook on high 1 hour
and then on low 1 to 2 hours or
until cheese is melted. Try not to
let soup boil.

Dawn's Four-Bean Turkey Chili

makes 10 servings
ideal slow cooker: 4-quart

1 lb. ground turkey, browned in
   non-stick skillet and drained
1 large onion, chopped
6-oz. can low-sodium tomato paste
2 Tbsp. chili powder
12-oz. can chili beans, undrained
12-oz. can kidney beans, undrained
12-oz. can black beans, undrained
12-oz. can pinto beans, undrained
12-oz. can low-sodium tomatoes
   with juice
Shredded low-fat Cheddar cheese
Fresh parsley (optional)

1. Combine ground turkey, onion,
and tomato paste in slow cooker.
2. Add chili powder, beans, and
tomatoes. Mix well.
3. Cover and cook on low 6 to 7
hours.
4. Serve with shredded low-fat
Cheddar cheese.
5. Sprinkle individual servings
with fresh parsley, if desired.

Gourmet White Chili

makes 8 servings
ideal slow cooker: 5-quart

1 lb. dried great Northern beans
2 medium onions, chopped
1 Tbsp. olive oil
4 garlic cloves, minced
8-oz. can chopped green chiles
2 tsp. ground cumin
2 tsp. dried oregano
¼ tsp. ground cloves
¼ tsp. cayenne pepper
2 lbs. boneless, skinless chicken
   breast halves, cubed
6 cups low-fat, low-sodium chicken
   broth
1 tsp. salt
½ tsp. black pepper
2 cups shredded low-fat or fat-free
   cheese, divided
Garnishes: 1 cup fat-free sour
   cream, 1 cup salsa, ½ cup
   chopped fresh cilantro

1. Cover dried beans with water
and soak overnight. Drain,
discarding soaking water.
2. Sauté onion in olive oil until
clear. Add garlic, green chiles,
cumin, oregano, cloves, and
cayenne pepper. Sauté 2 minutes
more. (This step may be skipped if
you are pressed for time.)
3. Place all ingredients except
cheese and garnishes in slow
cooker.
4. Cover and cook on high 4 to 6
hours or on high 1 hour and then
on low 6 to 8 hours.
5. Add 1 cup cheese. Stir until
melted.
6. Serve in bowls and top with
remaining 1 cup cheese; garnish,
if desired.

Black-Eyed Peas

Black-Eyed Peas

makes 4 to 5 servings
ideal slow cooker: 4- or 5-quart

1-lb. pkg. dried black-eyed peas
1½ cups diced cooked ham
6 cups hot water
½ tsp. salt
¼ tsp. pepper

1. Combine all ingredients in slow cooker.
2. Cover and cook on low 6 to 8 hours.

note:

• If your diet allows, consider adding 2 4-oz. cans diced green chiles, a pinch of red pepper flakes, or several drops of Tabasco sauce to Step 1.

Baked Corn

makes 8 servings
ideal slow cooker: 3-quart

4 cups corn (be sure to thaw and drain if using frozen corn)
2 eggs, beaten
1 tsp. salt
1 cup fat-free milk
⅛ tsp. pepper
2 tsp. oil
2 Tbsp. sugar
3 Tbsp. all-purpose flour

1. Spray slow cooker with cooking spray.
2. Combine all ingredients. Pour into slow cooker.
3. Cover and cook on high 3 hours.

Corn Bread Casserole

makes 8 servings
ideal slow cooker: 3- or 4-quart

1 qt. whole-kernel corn
1 qt. creamed corn
1 pkg. corn muffin mix
1 egg
2 Tbsp. butter
¼ tsp. garlic powder
2 Tbsp. sugar
¼ cup milk
½ tsp. salt
¼ tsp. pepper

1. Combine all ingredients in greased slow cooker.
2. Cover and cook on low 3½ to 4 hours, stirring once halfway through.

Vegetable Minestrone
(page 64)

healthy favorites

Fruit Salsa

makes 16 servings
ideal slow cooker: 2- or 3-quart

11-oz. can mandarin oranges
8½-oz. can unsweetened sliced
   peaches, undrained
8-oz. can unsweetened pineapple
   tidbits, undrained
1 medium onion, chopped
Half a medium-sized green bell
   pepper, chopped
Half a medium-sized red bell
pepper, chopped
Half a medium-sized yellow bell
   pepper, chopped
3 garlic cloves, minced
3 Tbsp. cornstarch
4 tsp. vinegar

1. Combine all ingredients in slow
cooker.
2. Cover and cook on high 2
hours, stirring occasionally.
3. Serve with baked tortilla chips.

Per Serving: Calories 35 (Calories from fat 0),
Total Fat 0g (Saturated Fat 0g), Cholesterol 0mg,
Sodium 5mg, Total Carbohydrate 8g, Dietary Fiber 0.5g,
Sugars 6g, Protein 0g

Slim Dunk

makes 12 servings
ideal slow cooker: 1½-quart

2 cups fat-free sour cream
¼ cup fat-free salad dressing
   (we used Miracle Whip)
10-oz. pkg. frozen chopped
   spinach, squeezed dry and
   chopped
1.8-oz. envelope dry leek soup mix
¼ cup minced red bell pepper

1. Combine all ingredients in slow
cooker. Mix well.
2. Cover and cook on high 1 hour.
3. Serve warm with fat-free baked
tortilla chips.

Per Serving: Calories 70 (Calories from fat 10),
Total Fat 1g, (Saturated Fat 0.5g), Cholesterol 5mg,
Sodium 310mg, Total Carbohydrate 11g, Dietary Fiber 0.5g,
Sugars 4g, Protein 3g

Pear Butter

makes 40 servings
ideal slow cooker: 4-quart

10 large pears (about 4 lbs.)
1 cup orange juice
1 cup sugar
Sugar substitute to equal ½ cup
1 tsp. ground cinnamon
1 tsp. ground cloves
½ tsp. ground allspice

1. Peel and quarter pears. Place in
slow cooker.
2. Cover and cook on low 10 to 12
hours. Drain and discard liquid.
3. Mash or puree pears. Add
remaining ingredients. Mix well
and return to slow cooker.
4. Cover and cook on high 1 hour.
5. Place in jars and chill. Store in
refrigerator.

Per Serving: Calories 56 (Calories from fat 2),
Total Fat 0g (Saturated Fat 0g), Cholesterol 0mg,
Sodium 0mg, Total Carbohydrate 14g, Dietary Fiber 1g,
Sugars 13g, Protein 0g

Boston Brown Bread

Boston Brown Bread

makes 8 servings
ideal slow cooker: 6-quart tall

½ cup all-purpose flour
½ tsp. baking powder
½ tsp. baking soda
½ tsp. salt
½ cup yellow cornmeal
½ cup whole wheat flour
¼ cup walnuts, chopped
6 Tbsp. unsulfured molasses
1 cup low-fat buttermilk or sour milk
½ cup raisins

1. Sift all-purpose flour with baking powder, baking soda, and salt.
2. Stir in cornmeal and whole wheat flour.
3. Add walnuts, molasses, buttermilk, and raisins. Beat well.
4. Pour batter into a lightly greased 1½-quart soufflé dish. Place rack in bottom of slow cooker.
5. Pour 1 cup water into slow cooker.
6. Place aluminum foil over top of dish, folding it down around the edge of the dish. Set soufflé dish inside cooker.

7. Cover and cook on high 2½ hours or until a skewer inserted in center of bread comes out clean.
8. Remove dish from cooker. Lay it on its side to cool. Keep dish covered 1 hour before unmolding.
9. Slice, and, if desired, serve with butter.

Per Serving: Calories 80 (Calories from Fat 10), Total Fat 1g (Saturated Fat 0g), Cholesterol 0g, Sodium 105mg, Total Carbohydrate 16g, Dietary Fiber 0.5g, Sugars 7g, Protein 2g

Coffee Beef Roast

makes 4 servings
ideal slow cooker: 4- or 5-quart

1½ lbs. boneless beef sirloin tip
  roast, cut in half
2 tsp. canola oil
1½ cups sliced fresh mushrooms
½ cup sliced green onions
2 garlic cloves, minced
1½ cups brewed coffee
1 tsp. liquid smoke (optional)
½ tsp. salt
½ tsp. chili powder
¼ tsp. pepper
¼ cup cornstarch
½ cup cold water

1. In a large non-stick skillet, brown roast over medium-high heat on all sides in oil. Transfer roast to slow cooker.
2. In the same skillet, sauté mushrooms, onions, and garlic until tender.
3. Stir coffee, liquid smoke if desired, salt, chili powder, and pepper into vegetables. Pour over roast.
4. Cover and cook on low 8 to 10 hours or until meat is tender.
5. Remove roast and keep warm.
6. Pour cooking juices into a 2-cup glass liquid measuring cup; skim fat.
7. Combine cornstarch and water in a saucepan until smooth. Gradually stir in 2 cups cooking juices.
8. Bring to a boil; cook and stir for 2 minutes or until thickened. Serve with sliced beef.

Per Serving: Calories 100 (Calories from Fat 30), Total Fat 3.5g (Saturated Fat 1g), Cholesterol 35mg, Sodium 120mg, Total Carbohydrate 4g, Dietary Fiber 0.5g, Sugars 1g, Protein 12g

---

editor's favorite

Texican Chili

makes 15 servings
ideal slow cooker: 5- or 6-quart

8 slices bacon, diced
2½ lbs. beef stewing meat, cubed
28-oz. can stewed tomatoes
14½-oz. can stewed tomatoes
8-oz. can tomato sauce
8-oz. can no-added-salt tomato
  sauce
16-oz. can kidney beans, rinsed
  and drained
2 cups sliced carrots
1 medium onion, chopped
1 cup chopped celery
½ cup chopped green bell pepper
¼ cup minced fresh parsley
1 Tbsp. chili powder
½ tsp. ground cumin
¼ tsp. black pepper

1. Cook bacon in skillet until crisp. Drain on paper towels.
2. Brown beef in bacon drippings in skillet.
3. Combine all ingredients in slow cooker.
4. Cover and cook on low 9 to 10 hours or until meat is tender. Stir occasionally.

Per Serving: Calories 165 (Calories from Fat 44), Total Fat 5g (Saturated Fat 1.5g), Cholesterol 40mg, Sodium 434mg, Total Carbohydrate 15g, Dietary Fiber 3g, Sugars 6g, Protein 16g

---

Easy Stuffed Shells

makes 7 servings
ideal slow cooker: 4-quart

20-oz. bag frozen stuffed shells,
  thawed
15-oz. can marinara or spaghetti
  sauce
15-oz. can green beans, drained

1. Place shells around edge of greased slow cooker.
2. Cover with marinara sauce.
3. Pour green beans in center.
4. Cover and cook on high 3 hours or on low 8 hours.
5. Serve with garlic toast and salad.

Per Serving: Calories 221 (Calories from Fat 66), Total Fat 7g (Saturated Fat 3.2g), Cholesterol 66mg, Sodium 728mg, Total Carbohydrate 27g, Dietary Fiber 3g, Sugars 7g, Protein 10g

---

Veggie Beef Stew

makes 5 servings
ideal slow cooker: 3- or 4-quart

¾ lb. beef stewing meat, trimmed
  of fat and cut in ½-inch cubes
2 tsp. canola oil
14½-oz. can low-sodium, low-fat
  beef broth
14½-oz. can low-sodium stewed
  tomatoes
1½ cups peeled and cubed
  butternut squash
1 cup fresh or thawed frozen corn
  kernels
½ cup chopped carrots
Dash of salt
Dash of pepper
Dash of dried oregano
2 Tbsp. cornstarch
¼ cup water

1. In a skillet, brown stewing meat in canola oil over medium heat. Transfer to slow cooker.
2. Add beef broth, vegetables, salt, pepper, and oregano.
3. Cover and cook on high 5 to 6 hours. Combine cornstarch and water until smooth. Stir into stew.
4. Cover and cook on high 30 minutes.

Per Serving: Calories 200 (Calories from Fat 50), Total Fat 5g (Saturated Fat 1.5g), Cholesterol 40mg, Sodium 180mg, Total Carbohydrate 22g, Dietary Fiber 4g, Sugars 6g, Protein 17g

Dawn's Harvest Pork Roast

makes 8 servings
ideal slow cooker: 4-quart

2 lbs. pork tenderloin, trimmed of fat
2 Tbsp. canola oil
3 cups apple juice
3 Granny Smith apples, sliced
1 cup fresh or frozen thawed cranberries
¾ tsp. salt
½ tsp. pepper

1. Brown roast on all sides in canola oil in skillet. Place in slow cooker.
2. Add remaining ingredients.
3. Cover and cook on low 6 to 8 hours.

Per Serving: Calories 290 (Calories from Fat 80), Total Fat 9g (Saturated Fat 2g), Cholesterol 90mg, Sodium 290mg, Total Carbohydrate 19g, Dietary Fiber 2g, Sugars 16g, Protein 32g

---

kid-friendly
Chunky Spaghetti Sauce

makes 16 servings
ideal slow cooker: 4-quart

1 lb. ground beef, browned and drained
½ lb. bulk sausage, browned and drained
14½-oz. can no-salt-added Italian tomatoes with basil
15-oz. can Italian tomato sauce
1 medium onion, chopped
1 green bell pepper, chopped
8-oz. can sliced mushrooms
½ cup dry red wine
2 tsp. sugar
1 tsp. minced garlic
1½ tsp. dried basil

1. Combine all ingredients in slow cooker.
2. Cover and cook on high 3½ to 4 hours or on low 7 to 8 hours.

Per Serving: Calories 134 (Calories from Fat 61), Total Fat 7g (Saturated Fat 2.5g), Cholesterol 30mg, Sodium 397mg, Total Carbohydrate 8g, Dietary Fiber 2g, Sugars 4g, Protein 11g

---

15-minute prep
Stew in a Snap

makes 6 servings
ideal slow cooker: 4-quart

Pick your favorite combination of frozen mixed vegetables for this heart-warming stew.

2 cups water
2 medium potatoes, diced
2.8-oz. envelope dry onion soup mix
16-oz. pkg. mixed frozen vegetables, thawed
1 lb. ground turkey, crumbled
4 slices bacon, diced and cooked until crisp
¼ tsp. pepper
2 garlic cloves, minced
1 Tbsp. sugar
1 Tbsp. all-purpose flour
28-oz. can chopped stewed tomatoes

1. Combine all ingredients in slow cooker.
2. Cover and cook on high 5 to 6 hours and then on low 2 to 3 hours.

Per Serving: Calories 280 (Calories from Fat 70), Total Fat 7g (Saturated Fat 2g), Cholesterol 45mg, Sodium 280mg, Total Carbohydrate 34g, Dietary Fiber 7g, Sugars 8g, Protein 21g

---

editor's favorite
Vegetable Minestrone

makes 12 servings
ideal slow cooker: 5-quart

pictured on page 60

4 cups low-fat, low-sodium vegetable broth
4 cups low-sodium tomato juice
1 Tbsp. dried basil
1 tsp. salt
½ tsp. dried oregano
¼ tsp. pepper
2 medium carrots, sliced
2 celery ribs, chopped
1 medium onion, chopped
1 cup sliced fresh mushrooms
2 garlic cloves, crushed
28-oz. can low-sodium diced tomatoes, undrained
1½ cups uncooked rotini pasta

1. Combine all ingredients except pasta in slow cooker.
2. Cover and cook on low 7 to 8 hours.
3. Add pasta.
4. Cover and cook on high 15 to 20 minutes. Sprinkle each serving with shredded Parmesan cheese, if you like. Serve with cheese garlic toast.

Per Serving: Calories 70 (Calories from Fat 0), Total Fat 0g (Saturated Fat 0g), Cholesterol 0mg, Sodium 520 mg, Total Carbohydrate 13g, Dietary Fiber 3g, Sugars 6g, Protein 5g

Black and Blue Cobbler

makes 12 servings
ideal slow cooker: 5-quart

1 cup all-purpose flour

6 Tbsp. sugar

Sugar substitute to equal 3 Tbsp.

1 tsp. baking powder

¼ tsp. salt

¼ tsp. ground cinnamon

¼ tsp. ground nutmeg

2 eggs, beaten

2 Tbsp. milk

2 Tbsp. vegetable oil

2 cups fresh or frozen blueberries

2 cups fresh or frozen blackberries

¾ cup water

1 tsp. grated orange peel

6 Tbsp. sugar

Sugar substitute to equal 3 Tbsp.

Whipped topping or ice cream
  (optional)

1. Combine flour, 6 Tbsp. sugar, sugar substitute to equal 3 Tbsp., baking powder, salt, cinnamon, and nutmeg.

2. Combine eggs, milk, and oil. Stir into dry ingredients until moistened.

3. Spread batter evenly over bottom of greased slow cooker.

4. In saucepan, combine berries, water, orange peel, 6 Tbsp. sugar, and sugar substitute to equal 3 Tbsp. Bring to a boil. Remove from heat and pour over batter.

5. Cover and cook on high 2 to 2½ hours or until toothpick inserted into batter comes out clean. Turn off cooker.

6. Uncover and let stand 30 minutes before serving. Spoon from cooker and serve with whipped topping or ice cream, if desired.

Per Serving: Calories 170 (Calories from Fat 31), Total Fat 3g (Saturated Fat 0.5g), Cholesterol 36mg, Sodium 92mg, Total Carbohydrate 34g, Dietary Fiber 2g, Sugars 23g, Protein 3g

Breakfast Casserole (page 69)

breakfast and brunch

Breakfast Wassail

makes 4 quarts
ideal slow cooker: 5-quart

....

Even though this recipe conjures thoughts of Christmas, it's the perfect anytime breakfast substitute for juice, especially when entertaining a houseful of overnight guests.

64-oz. bottle cranberry juice
32-oz. bottle apple juice
12-oz. can frozen pineapple juice
   concentrate
12-oz. can frozen lemonade
   concentrate
3 to 4 cinnamon sticks
1 qt. water (optional)

1. Combine all ingredients except water in a slow cooker. Add water, if desired, if mixture is too sweet.
2. Cover and cook on low 3 hours. Serve from cooker.

Spiced Coffee

makes 8 servings
ideal slow cooker: 3-quart

....

8 cups brewed coffee
⅓ cup sugar
¼ cup low-fat chocolate syrup
½ tsp. anise extract
4 cinnamon sticks, halved
1½ tsp. whole cloves

1. Combine coffee, sugar, chocolate syrup, and anise extract in slow cooker.
2. Place cinnamon sticks and cloves in a cheesecloth bag. Place in slow cooker.
3. Cover and cook on low 2 to 3 hours.
4. Discard spice bag.
5. Ladle coffee into mugs.

Peach or Apricot Butter

makes 48 2-Tbsp. servings
ideal slow cooker: 4-quart

....

4 1-lb., 13-oz. cans peaches or
   apricots
1½ cups sugar
Sugar substitute to equal ¾ cup
2 tsp. ground cinnamon
1 tsp. ground cloves

1. Drain fruit. Remove pits. Puree fruit in blender. Pour into slow cooker.
2. Stir in remaining ingredients.
3. Cover and cook on high 8 to 10 hours. Remove cover during last half of cooking. Stir occasionally.

note:

• Spread on bread or use to top ice cream or pound cake.

Apple Butter
for Your Toast

Mexican-Style Grits

makes 10 to 12 servings
ideal slow cooker: 4-quart

1½ cups dry instant grits
1 lb. loaf process cheese spread,
    cubed
½ tsp. garlic powder
2 4.5-oz. cans diced chiles
½ cup (1 stick) butter or margarine

1. Prepare grits according to package directions.
2. Stir in cheese, garlic powder, and chiles until cheese is melted.
3. Stir in butter. Pour into greased slow cooker.
4. Cover and cook on high 2 to 3 hours or on low 4 to 6 hours.

Apple Oatmeal

makes 4 to 5 servings
ideal slow cooker: 3-quart

2 cups fat-free milk
1 Tbsp. honey
1 Tbsp. light, soft tub margarine
¼ tsp. salt
½ tsp. ground cinnamon
1 cup dry regular oats
1 cup chopped apples
½ cup chopped walnuts
1½ Tbsp. brown sugar

1. Mix together all ingredients in greased slow cooker.
2. Cover and cook on low 5 to 6 hours.
3. Serve with milk or ice cream.

variation:

: • Add ½ cup light or dark raisins
: to mixture to Step 1.

Apple Butter for Your Toast

makes 9 cups
ideal slow cooker: 5- or 6-quart

"Where's the toast?" is what you'll hear from family and friends when they smell this treat cooking in the kitchen. This apple butter also tastes wonderful on plain yogurt.

108-oz. can (#8 size) unsweetened
    applesauce (about 12 cups)
2 cups apple cider
1 Tbsp. ground cinnamon
1 tsp. ground ginger
½ tsp. ground cloves or 1 tsp.
    ground nutmeg (optional)

1. Combine applesauce and cider in slow cooker.
2. Cover and cook on high 3 to 4 hours.
3. Add spices.
4. Cover and cook 1 hour more.
5. Fill jars with apple butter. Cover and refrigerate up to 2 weeks.

note:

: • This apple butter yields a lot so
: it's perfect for gift-giving. Attach
: a gift card explaining to store it
: in the refrigerator up to 2 weeks
: (including the time since you
: made it).

Hot Wheat Berry Cereal

makes 4 servings
ideal slow cooker: 4-quart

1 cup wheat berries
5 cups water
Butter
Milk
Honey

1. Rinse and sort berries. Place in slow cooker and add water. Soak all day (or 8 hours) in slow cooker.
2. Cover and cook on low 10 hours or overnight.
3. Drain, if needed. Serve hot with butter, milk, and honey.

variation:

: • Eat your hot wheat berries with raisins and maple syrup.

kid-friendly

Egg and Cheese Bake

makes 6 servings
ideal slow cooker: 4-quart

3 cups toasted bread cubes
1½ cups shredded reduced-fat sharp Cheddar cheese
Fried, crumbled bacon or ham chunks (optional)
4 eggs, beaten
4 egg whites
3 cups fat-free milk
¼ tsp. pepper

1. Combine bread cubes, cheese, and, if desired, meat in greased slow cooker.
2. Mix together eggs, egg whites, milk, and pepper. Pour over bread.
3. Cover and cook on high 2 to 3 hours.

Cornmeal Mush

makes 10 servings
ideal slow cooker: 3½- or 4-quart

Enjoy a bowl of hot mush for breakfast or supper with milk and sugar. Pour leftovers into a container to cool and refrigerate overnight. To reheat, slice and brown in a skillet until golden on each side and serve with apple butter or maple syrup.

2 cups cornmeal
5 cups cold water, divided
1½ tsp. salt
1 Tbsp. butter or margarine

1. In a mixing bowl, stir together cornmeal, 2 cups cold water, and salt. When smooth, add remaining water and butter. Stir well.
2. Spray slow cooker with cooking spray. Pour cornmeal mixture into slow cooker.
3. Cover and cook on low 7 to 8 hours.

Breakfast Casserole

makes 8 to 10 servings
ideal slow cooker: 4-quart

pictured on page 66

6 eggs, beaten
1½ lbs. bulk sausage, browned and drained
1½ cups milk
1 cup shredded Cheddar cheese
8 slices bread, torn into pieces
1 tsp. salt
½ tsp. dry mustard
1 cup shredded mozzarella cheese

1. Stir together all ingredients except mozzarella cheese. Pour into greased slow cooker.
2. Sprinkle mozzarella cheese over top.
3. Cover and cook on high 2 hours and then on low 1 hour.

note:

• Spoon this yummy casserole straight out of the cooker onto serving plates. Or, for a fancier presentation, spoon into individual dishes.

kid-friendly

Western Omelet Casserole

makes 10 servings
ideal slow cooker: 4- or 5-quart

32-oz. bag frozen hash brown potatoes, thawed
1 lb. cooked ham, cubed
1 medium onion, diced
1½ cups shredded Cheddar cheese
12 eggs
1 cup milk
1 tsp. salt
1 tsp. pepper

1. Layer one-third each of potatoes, ham, onion, and cheese in slow cooker. Repeat 2 times.
2. Beat together eggs, milk, salt, and pepper. Pour over mixture in slow cooker.
3. Cover and cook on high 1 hour and then on low 6 to 7 hours.
4. Serve with orange juice and fresh fruit.

Welsh Rarebit

Welsh Rarebit

makes 16 servings
ideal slow cooker: 3- or 4-quart

12-oz. can beer
1 Tbsp. dry mustard
1 tsp. Worcestershire sauce
⅛ tsp. black pepper or white
    pepper
8 ozs. reduced-fat American
    cheese, cubed
8 ozs. reduced-fat sharp
    Cheddar cheese, cubed
English muffins or toast
Tomato slices
Bacon, cooked until crisp
Fresh steamed asparagus spears

1. Combine beer, mustard,
Worcestershire sauce, and pepper
in slow cooker.
2. Cover and cook on high 1 to 2
hours or until mixture boils.
3. Add cheeses, a little at a time,
stirring constantly until all the
cheese melts.
4. Heat on high 20 to 30 minutes
with cover off, stirring frequently.
5. Layer toasted English muffins
with tomato slices, strips of crisp
bacon, and asparagus spears. Top
with cheese sauce.

kid-friendly

Dulce de Leche
(Sweet Milk)

makes 1¼ cups
ideal slow cooker: 3- or 4-quart

14-oz. can sweetened condensed
    milk

1. Pour milk into a 2-cup glass
measuring cup; cover with foil.
Place in slow cooker.
2. Add very hot water to cooker
to reach level of milk in glass
measuring cup. Cover and cook
on low 9 hours (milk should be
the color of caramel).

note:

• This dish often appears on
Mexican menus. Enjoy it at
breakfast spooned over toast
or pancakes. To make a divine
pie, spoon the entire recipe into
a 6-oz. graham cracker crust
and top it with an 8-oz. carton
frozen thawed whipped topping
and then the candy bar of your
choice, chopped.

healthy for you

Breakfast Fruit Compote

makes 8 to 9 servings
ideal slow cooker: 3- or 4-quart

12-oz. pkg. dried apricots
12-oz. pkg. pitted dried plums
11-oz. can mandarin oranges in
    light syrup, undrained
29-oz. can sliced peaches in light
    syrup, undrained
¼ cup white raisins
10 maraschino cherries

1. Combine all ingredients in slow
cooker. Mix well.
2. Cover and cook on high 2 to 3
hours or on low 6 to 7 hours.

note:

• If the fruit seems to be drying
out as it cooks, you may want to
add up to 1 cup water.

healthy for you • kid-friendly

Blueberry Apple
Waffle Topping

makes 10 to 12 servings
ideal slow cooker: 3½- or 4-quart

4 cups natural applesauce,
    unsweetened
2 Granny Smith apples, unpeeled,
    cored, and sliced
1 pt. fresh or thawed frozen
    blueberries
1½ Tbsp. ground cinnamon
½ cup pure maple syrup
1 tsp. almond flavoring
½ cup walnuts, chopped

1. Stir together applesauce, apples,
and blueberries in slow cooker
sprayed with cooking spray.
2. Add cinnamon and maple syrup.
3. Cover and cook on low 3 hours.
4. Add almond flavoring and
walnuts just before serving.

note:

• If your diet allows, this is also
delicious served over cake or fat-
free frozen yogurt.

Cranberry-Orange Muffins (page 76)

rounding out the meal

for the holidays
Garlic-Cheese Grits

makes 18 servings

This dish can be made about 1 hour before a party; it reheats perfectly over low heat.

7 cups water
2¼ tsp. salt
2 cups uncooked regular grits
3 garlic cloves, minced
1-lb. loaf process cheese spread, cubed
½ cup half-and-half
⅓ cup butter or margarine

1. Bring water and salt to a boil in a large Dutch oven; gradually stir in grits and garlic. Cover, reduce heat, and simmer, stirring occasionally, 8 minutes.
2. Add cheese, half-and-half, and butter; simmer, stirring constantly, until cheese and butter melt.

make-ahead
Green Pea Salad

makes 4 to 6 servings

16-oz. can small sweet green peas, drained
16-oz. can medium-sized sweet green peas, drained
6 green onions, sliced
2 hard-cooked eggs, chopped
¾ cup diced sharp Cheddar cheese
½ cup mayonnaise
1 tsp. sugar
1 tsp. minced fresh dill
1 tsp. lemon juice
¼ tsp. salt
¼ tsp. pepper

1. Stir together all ingredients in a large bowl. Cover and chill until ready to serve.

Cantaloupe Salad

makes 4 servings

½ cup mayonnaise
3 Tbsp. frozen orange juice concentrate, thawed and undiluted
1 small cantaloupe, chilled
Leaf lettuce
1⅓ cups seedless green or red grapes

1. Stir together mayonnaise and orange juice concentrate.
2. Cut cantaloupe into 4 sections; remove seeds and peel. Place cantaloupe sections on lettuce-lined plates. Top with grapes; drizzle with mayonnaise mixture.

Presto Pasta Salad

lemon-dill vinaigrette

makes ¾ cup

¼ cup lemon juice
1 tsp. dried dill weed
1 tsp. garlic salt
½ cup olive oil

1. Whisk together all ingredients.

Garden Rice

makes 2 servings

1 Tbsp. butter or margarine
2 green onions, sliced
1 small zucchini, chopped
½ red bell pepper, seeded and
    chopped
½ cup long-grain rice, uncooked
1 Tbsp. dried parsley flakes
½ tsp. chicken bouillon granules
¼ tsp. salt
1 cup water

1. Melt butter in a saucepan; add green onions, zucchini, and red pepper. Cook over medium-high heat, stirring constantly, until crisp-tender. Add rice and remaining ingredients; bring to a boil. Cover, reduce heat, and cook 15 minutes or until water is absorbed and rice is tender.

make-ahead
Presto Pasta Salad

makes 4 servings

8 ozs. dried rotini pasta
1½ cups broccoli florets
1 cup sliced fresh mushrooms
1 large red bell pepper, seeded
    and cut into 1-inch pieces
8-oz. bottle Caesar salad dressing

1. Cook pasta according to package directions; drain. Rinse with cold water; drain and place in a large bowl.
2. Add broccoli and remaining ingredients to pasta; toss well to coat ingredients with dressing. Cover and chill, if desired.

Green Salad with Lemon-Dill Vinaigrette

makes 6 servings

14.8-oz. jar hearts of palm, drained
1 red onion
1 roasted red bell pepper, drained
6 cups mixed baby lettuces
Lemon-Dill Vinaigrette
Shaved Parmesan cheese

1. Cut hearts of palm into ½-inch slices. Cut onion in half lengthwise; slice and separate into strips. Cut red pepper into thin strips.
2. Combine baby lettuce, hearts of palm, onion, and pepper strips in a large salad bowl; toss with Lemon-Dill Vinaigrette. Top with Parmesan cheese and serve immediately.

Mashed Potatoes with Tomato Gravy

makes 6 to 8 servings

22-oz. pkg. frozen mashed
    potatoes
2⅓ cups milk
½ 8-oz. pkg. cream cheese, softened
1 tsp. salt
1 tsp. seasoned pepper
Tomato Gravy

1. Stir together potatoes and milk in a large microwave-safe bowl. Microwave at HIGH 8 minutes; stir and microwave 5 to 7 minutes more. Let stand 2 minutes.

2. Stir in cream cheese, salt, and seasoned pepper, stirring until cheese melts and mixture is blended. Serve with Tomato Gravy.

note:

> • To lighten, use fat-free milk and reduced-fat cream cheese.

tomato gravy

makes 2½ cups

2 Tbsp. butter or margarine
2 Tbsp. all-purpose flour
½ cup chicken broth
14½-oz. can diced tomatoes with basil, oregano, and garlic
1 tsp. sugar
½ tsp. seasoned pepper

1. Melt butter in large saucepan over medium heat; add flour, stirring until smooth. Cook, stirring constantly, 1 minute. Add broth, stirring until smooth.

2. Add diced tomatoes, sugar, and pepper. Cook, stirring often, 3 to 5 minutes or until thickened.

kid-friendly

Parmesan-Crusted Potato Wedges

makes 6 servings

¼ cup grated Parmesan cheese
¼ cup all-purpose flour
1 tsp. garlic salt
½ tsp. salt
¼ tsp. pepper
6 medium potatoes, unpeeled
½ cup butter or margarine

1. Combine first 5 ingredients in a large heavy-duty, zip-top plastic bag. Cut potatoes lengthwise into fourths; add potato wedges to bag, and shake gently to coat. Set aside.

2. Place butter in a 15- x 10- x 1-inch jellyroll pan lined with aluminum foil. Place pan in a 425° oven until butter melts. Spread potato wedges in a single layer in pan, and return to oven. Bake, uncovered, 30 minutes, turning wedges after 15 minutes.

Buttermilk-Fried Corn

makes 2 cups

2 cups fresh corn kernels
1½ cups buttermilk
⅔ cup all-purpose flour
⅔ cup cornmeal
1 tsp. salt
½ tsp. pepper
Corn oil

1. Combine corn kernels and buttermilk in large bowl; let stand 30 minutes. Drain.

2. Combine flour and next 3 ingredients in large zip-top plastic bag. Add corn to flour mixture, a small amount at a time, and shake bag to coat corn.

3. Pour oil to depth of 1 inch in a Dutch oven; heat to 375°. Fry corn, a small amount at a time, in hot oil 2 minutes or until golden. Drain on paper towels. Serve as a side dish or sprinkle on salads, soups, or casseroles.

Okra Creole

makes 4 servings

3 slices bacon
16-oz. pkg. frozen sliced okra
14.5-oz. can chopped tomatoes
1 cup frozen onion seasoning blend
1 cup frozen corn kernels
½ cup water
1 tsp. Creole seasoning
¼ tsp. pepper

1. Cook bacon in a Dutch oven until crisp; remove bacon and drain on paper towels, reserving drippings. Crumble bacon and set aside.

2. Cook okra and next 6 ingredients in hot drippings in Dutch oven over medium-high heat, stirring occasionally, 5 minutes. Reduce heat to low, cover, and simmer 15 minutes or until vegetables are tender. Top with crumbled bacon. Serve over rice, if desired.

Tasty Black-Eyed Peas

makes 6 servings

4 bacon slices
1 medium-sized green bell pepper, seeded and chopped
1 medium onion, chopped
2 15.8-oz. cans black-eyed peas, drained
14½-oz. can Cajun-style stewed tomatoes, undrained and chopped
½ tsp. salt
¼ tsp. pepper

1. Cook bacon in a large skillet until crisp and remove bacon, reserving drippings in skillet. Crumble bacon and set aside.
2. Cook green pepper and onion in bacon drippings over medium-high heat, stirring constantly, until tender. Add peas and remaining 3 ingredients to skillet. Cook over low heat until thoroughly heated, stirring often. Sprinkle with bacon.

Basic Corn Bread

makes 6 servings

You can freeze this favorite in a zip-top freezer bag up to 1 month. Thaw it in the refrigerator when ready to serve.

⅓ cup butter
2 cups white cornmeal mix
¾ cup all-purpose flour
1 Tbsp. sugar
2¼ cups buttermilk
2 large eggs

1. Place butter in a 10-inch cast-iron skillet and heat in a 425° oven 5 minutes or until just melted.
2. Combine cornmeal mix, flour, and sugar in a large bowl.
3. Stir together buttermilk and eggs. Add to dry ingredients; stir just until moistened. Pour over melted butter in skillet.
4. Bake at 425° for 25 minutes or until golden. Cut in wedges to serve.

note:

- For testing purposes only, we used White Lily White Cornmeal Mix.

for the holidays • kid-friendly

Cranberry-Orange Muffins

makes 1 dozen

pictured on page 72

2 cups self-rising flour
¾ cup sweetened dried cranberries
½ cup sugar
1 Tbsp. grated orange rind
1 cup milk
¼ cup vegetable oil
2 large eggs

1. Combine first 4 ingredients in a large bowl; make a well in center of mixture.
2. Whisk together milk, oil, and eggs until well blended. Add to flour mixture and stir just until dry ingredients are moistened.
3. Spoon mixture into lightly greased muffin pans, filling two-thirds full.
4. Bake at 400° for 15 to 18 minutes or until golden brown. Remove from pans immediately.

Quick Biscuits

makes 1 dozen

⅔ cup sour cream
⅔ cup club soda
2 Tbsp. sugar
4 cups biscuit and baking mix

1. Combine first 3 ingredients in a large bowl, stirring well. Add biscuit mix, stirring just until dry ingredients are moistened.
2. Turn dough out onto a lightly floured surface; knead 3 or 4 times.
3. Shape dough into 12 biscuits (about 1-inch thick). Place 1 biscuit each in centers of two lightly greased 8-inch round cake pans. Arrange remaining biscuits in a circle around center biscuits.
4. Bake at 450° for 13 minutes or until golden.

Cheddar Biscuits

makes 8 biscuits

1 cup biscuit and baking mix
½ cup shredded sharp Cheddar cheese
¼ to ⅓ cup milk

1. Combine biscuit mix and cheese; add milk, stirring just until dry ingredients are moistened. (Dough will be very soft.) Turn dough out onto a floured surface; knead lightly 3 or 4 times.
2. Roll dough to ½-inch thickness; cut into rounds with a 2-inch biscuit cutter. Place biscuits on a lightly greased baking sheet.
3. Bake at 450° for 10 minutes or until golden. Serve immediately.

Pecan Pie with
Hot Fudge Sauce

1. Prepare cake mix according to package directions, using 1 cup water and ⅓ cup orange juice instead of liquid called for on package directions. Stir in orange extract. Spoon batter into an ungreased 10-inch tube pan.

2. Bake at 350° on lowest oven rack for 40 to 45 minutes or until cake springs back when lightly touched. Invert pan over neck of a glass bottle; let cool completely. Loosen cake from sides of pan, and remove from pan.

variations:

• For Chocolate Angel Food Cake, omit water, juice, and extract. Combine cake mix and ¼ cup sifted unsweetened cocoa powder. Prepare cake according to package directions.

• For Lemon Angel Food Cake, omit orange juice and extract, and substitute ¼ cup frozen lemon juice concentrate, thawed, and 2 tsp. grated lemon rind.

• For Peppermint Angel Food Cake, omit water, orange juice, and extract. Prepare cake mix according to package directions, stirring 5 hard peppermint candies, crushed, and ¼ tsp. peppermint extract into batter.

• For Coconut Angel Food Cake, omit water, orange juice, and extract. Prepare cake mix according to package directions, folding ½ cup flaked coconut, toasted, and ¼ tsp. coconut extract into batter.

5 ingredients or less

Pecan Pie with Hot Fudge Sauce

makes 6 to 8 servings

Homemade hot fudge sauce dresses up a simple frozen pie.

2-lb., 4-oz. pkg. frozen Mrs. Smith's Special Recipe Southern Pecan Pie
2 14-oz. cans sweetened condensed milk
1 cup semisweet chocolate morsels
2 tsp. vanilla extract
Dash of salt
Cinnamon-flavored ice cream (optional)

1. Remove and discard paper circle from pecan pie.

2. Thaw pie at room temperature for 2 hours.

3. Cook condensed milk and next 3 ingredients in a heavy saucepan over medium-low heat, stirring constantly, 4 to 6 minutes or until smooth. Serve warm over pie. Serve pie with ice cream, if desired.

Orange Angel Food Cake

makes 1 10-inch cake

16-oz. pkg. angel food cake mix (we used Duncan Hines)
1 cup water
⅓ cup orange juice
1 tsp. orange extract or flavoring

Page 131

Page 96

Page 154

Page 127

slow-cooker cookbook

All-American Snack

appetizers and beverages

All-American Snack

makes 3 quarts
ideal slow cooker: 6-quart

3 cups thin pretzel sticks
4 cups Wheat Chex
4 cups Cheerios
12-oz. can cocktail peanuts
¼ cup butter or margarine, melted
1 tsp. garlic powder
1 tsp. celery salt
½ tsp. seasoned salt
2 Tbsp. grated Parmesan cheese

1. Combine pretzels, cereal, and peanuts in a large bowl.
2. Combine butter, garlic powder, celery salt, seasoned salt, and Parmesan cheese. Pour over pretzels and cereal. Toss until blended.
3. Pour into slow cooker. Cover and cook on low 2½ hours, stirring every 30 minutes. Remove lid and cook another 30 minutes on low.
4. Serve warm or at room temperature. Store in an airtight container.

variation:

• Use 3 cups Wheat Chex (instead of 4 cups) and 3 cups Cheerios (instead of 4 cups). Add 3 cups Corn Chex.

kid-friendly

Barbecue Smokies

makes 8 to 10 servings
ideal slow cooker: 4-quart

2 lbs. cocktail-size smoked sausages
18-oz. bottle barbecue sauce
(your choice of flavors)

1. Place sausages in slow cooker.
2. Pour barbecue sauce over sausages.
3. Cover and cook on low 3 to 4 hours.

Curried Almonds

makes 4 cups
ideal slow cooker: 2-quart

1 lb. blanched almonds
2 Tbsp. melted butter
1 Tbsp. curry powder
½ tsp. seasoned salt

1. Place almonds in slow cooker.
2. Combine butter, curry powder, and seasoned salt. Pour over almonds. Stir to coat well.
3. Cover and cook on low 2 to 3 hours. Turn heat to high. Uncover and cook 1 to 1½ hours, stirring occasionally. Serve hot or cold.

Seafood Dip

15-minute prep

Seafood Dip

makes 12 servings
ideal slow cooker: 3½-quart

8-oz. pkg. cream cheese
8-oz. pkg. imitation crabmeat, chopped
2 Tbsp. finely chopped onion
4 to 5 drops hot sauce
¼ cup finely chopped walnuts
1 tsp. paprika

1. Blend all ingredients except nuts and paprika until well mixed.
2. Spread in slow cooker. Sprinkle with nuts and paprika.
3. Cover and cook on low 3 hours. Serve warm with crackers and bell pepper strips.

Chili con Queso

makes 12 to 16 servings
ideal slow cooker: 2-quart

1 medium onion, chopped
2 Tbsp. oil
2 4-oz. cans chopped green chiles
14½-oz. can Mexican-style stewed tomatoes, drained
1 lb. Velveeta cheese, cubed

1. Sauté onion in oil in skillet until transparent. Add chiles and tomatoes. Bring to a boil.
2. Add cheese. Pour into slow cooker. Cover and cook on low 2 hours.
3. Keep warm in cooker, stirring occasionally.
4. Serve with tortilla chips.

5 ingredients or less

Chili Nuts

makes 80 servings
ideal slow cooker: 3-quart

¼ cup melted butter
2 12-oz. cans cocktail peanuts
1⅝-oz. pkg. chili seasoning mix

1. Pour butter over nuts in slow cooker. Sprinkle in dry chili mix. Toss together.
2. Cover and cook on low 2 to 2½ hours. Remove lid and cook on high 10 to 15 minutes.
3. Serve warm or cool.

editor's favorite

Cheese Dip

makes 12 to 15 servings
ideal slow cooker: 3-quart

1 lb. white American cheese, sliced
1½ cups milk

1. Combine cheese and milk in slow cooker.
2. Cover and cook on low about 2 hours or until cheese is melted, stirring occasionally.
3. Serve with tortilla chips.

Cocktail Meatballs

Cocktail Meatballs

makes 10 to 12 servings
ideal slow cooker: 4-quart

3 lbs. ground chuck

1-oz. envelope dry onion soup mix

14-oz. can sweetened condensed
milk

18-oz. bottle ketchup

½ cup brown sugar

¼ cup Worcestershire sauce

1. Combine beef, soup mix, and
condensed milk. Form into about
3 dozen meatballs, each about
1½-inch round.

2. Place meatballs on a baking
sheet. Brown in 350° oven for 30
minutes. Remove from oven and
drain. Place meatballs in slow
cooker.

3. Combine ketchup, brown sugar,
and Worcestershire sauce. Pour
over meatballs.

4. Cover and cook on low 3 to
4 hours. Serve with decorative
wooden picks.

Hamburger-Cheese Dip

makes 20 servings
ideal slow cooker: 1-quart

¾ lb. ground beef, browned and
    crumbled into small pieces
⅛ tsp. salt
½ cup chopped green bell pepper
¾ cup chopped onion
8-oz. can no-sugar-added tomato
    sauce
4-oz. can green chiles, chopped
1 Tbsp. Worcestershire sauce
1 Tbsp. brown sugar
8 ozs. Velveeta Light cheese, cubed
1 Tbsp. paprika
Red pepper

1. Combine beef, salt, bell pepper,
onion, tomato sauce, green chiles,
Worcestershire sauce, and brown
sugar in slow cooker.
2. Cover and cook on low 2 to 3
hours. During the last hour, stir in
cheese, paprika, and red pepper.
3. Serve with tortilla chips.

5 ingredients or less

Refried Bean Dip

makes 12 servings
ideal slow cooker: 3-quart

20-oz. can fat-free refried beans
1 cup shredded fat-free Cheddar
    cheese
½ cup chopped green onions
2 to 4 Tbsp. bottled taco sauce to
    taste

1. Combine beans, cheese, onions,
and taco sauce in slow cooker.
2. Cover and cook on high 30
minutes and then on low 30
minutes or on low 2 to 2½ hours.
3. Serve with tortilla chips.

Quick-and-Easy Nacho Dip

makes 20 servings
ideal slow cooker: 3-quart

½ lb. 85%-lean ground beef
Salt (optional)
Pepper (optional)
Onion powder (optional)
2 garlic cloves, minced (optional)
2 16-oz. jars salsa (as hot or mild as
    you like)
15-oz. can fat-free refried beans
1½ cups fat-free sour cream
1½ cups shredded reduced-fat
    sharp Cheddar cheese, divided

1. Brown ground beef in skillet.
Drain. Add salt, pepper, onion powder, and minced garlic, if desired.
2. Combine beef mixture, salsa,
beans, sour cream, and 1 cup
cheese in slow cooker.
3. Cover and cook on low 2 hours.
Just before serving, sprinkle with
remaining ½ cup cheese.

5 ingredients or less

Reuben Dip

makes 8 to 12 servings
ideal slow cooker: 3- or 4-quart

8-oz. carton sour cream
2 8-oz. pkgs. cream cheese,
    softened
8-oz. can sauerkraut, drained
3 2½-oz. pkgs. dried corned beef,
    finely chopped
6-oz. pkg. shredded Swiss cheese

1. Combine all ingredients in slow
cooker.
2. Cover and cook on low 3 to 4
hours or until cheeses are melted.
3. Serve from cooker with rye
crackers or rye party bread.

Championship Bean Dip

makes 18 servings
ideal slow cooker: 3-quart

15-oz. can refried beans
1 cup picante sauce
1 cup shredded Monterey Jack
    cheese
1 cup shredded Cheddar cheese
¾ cup sour cream
3-oz. pkg. cream cheese, softened
1 Tbsp. chili powder
¼ tsp. ground cumin

1. Combine all ingredients in a
bowl. Transfer to slow cooker.
2. Cover and cook on high 2 hours
or until heated through, stirring
once or twice.
3. Serve warm with tortilla chips
and salsa.

Hot Crab Dip

makes 20 servings
ideal slow cooker: 2-quart

⅓ cup salsa
½ cup fat-free milk
2 8-oz. pkgs. imitation crabmeat,
    finely flaked
¾ cup thinly sliced green onions
4.5-oz. can chopped green chiles
3 8-oz. pkgs. fat-free cream cheese,
    cubed

1. Spray slow cooker with cooking
spray.
2. Stir together salsa and milk in a
large bowl.
3. Stir in remaining ingredients.
Pour into slow cooker.
4. Cover and cook on low 3 to
4 hours, stirring approximately
every 30 minutes.
5. Serve warm with crackers.

Stuffed Mushrooms

makes 6 servings
ideal slow cooker: 3½-quart oval

14 large mushrooms
1 Tbsp. canola oil
¼ tsp. minced garlic
Dash of salt
Dash of black pepper
Dash of cayenne pepper
¼ cup grated reduced-fat
    Monterey Jack cheese
Garnish: Italian parsley sprigs

1. Remove stems from mushrooms and dice stems. Dice 2 mushrooms.
2. Heat oil in skillet. Sauté diced mushrooms, stems, and garlic until softened. Remove skillet from heat.
3. Stir in seasonings and cheese. Stuff into mushroom shells. Place in slow cooker in a single layer.
4. Cover and cook on low 1½ to 2 hours.
5. Transfer mushrooms to a serving platter using a slotted spoon. Garnish with Italian parsley.

variations:

  • Add 1 Tbsp. minced onion to Step 2.
  • Use Monterey Jack cheese with jalapeños instead of regular.

Stuffed Mushrooms

Artichokes

makes 4 servings
ideal slow cooker: 4-quart oval

4 artichokes
1 tsp. salt
2 Tbsp. lemon juice
Melted butter

1. Wash and trim artichokes by cutting off the stems flush with the bottoms of the artichokes and by cutting ¾ to 1 inch off the tops. Stand upright in slow cooker.
2. Stir together salt and lemon juice and pour over artichokes. Pour in enough water to cover three-fourths of artichokes.
3. Cover and cook on high 2 to 4 hours or on low 8 to 10 hours.
4. Serve with melted butter. Pull off individual leaves and dip bottom of each into butter. Using your teeth, strip the individual leaf of the meaty portion at the bottom of each leaf.

TNT Dip

makes 8 cups
ideal slow cooker: 3- or 4-quart

1½ lbs. ground beef, browned
10¾-oz. can cream of mushroom
    soup
¼ cup butter, melted
1 lb. Velveeta cheese, cubed
1 cup salsa
2 Tbsp. chili powder

1. Combine all ingredients in slow cooker.
2. Cover and cook on high 1 to 1¼ hours or until cheese is melted, stirring occasionally.
3. Serve with tortilla chips, corn chips, or party rye bread.

variation:

  • To change the balance of flavors, use 1 lb. browned ground beef and 1½ cups salsa.

Cheesy New Orleans Shrimp Dip

makes 14 servings
ideal slow cooker: 3-quart

1 bacon slice
3 medium onions, chopped
1 garlic clove, minced
4 jumbo shrimp, peeled and
    deveined
1 medium tomato, peeled and
    chopped
3 cups shredded Monterey Jack
    cheese
4 drops Tabasco sauce
⅛ tsp. cayenne pepper
Dash of black pepper

1. Cook bacon in skillet until crisp. Drain on paper towel, reserving drippings in skillet. Crumble bacon.
2. Sauté onion and garlic in bacon drippings. Drain on a paper towel.
3. Coarsely chop shrimp.
4. Combine all ingredients in slow cooker.
5. Cover and cook on low 1 hour or until cheese is melted. (Thin with milk if too thick.) Serve warm with chips.

Homestyle Tomato Juice

makes 4 to 5 servings
ideal slow cooker: 5-quart

10 to 12 large tomatoes
1 tsp. salt
1 tsp. seasoned salt
¼ tsp. pepper
1 Tbsp. sugar

1. Wash and drain tomatoes. Remove cores and blossom ends. Place in slow cooker.

2. Cover and cook on low 4 to 6 hours or until tomatoes are soft.
3. Press through sieve or food mill.
4. Stir in seasonings. Chill.

for the holidays
Spiced Cider

makes 12 servings
ideal slow cooker: 5-quart

12 whole cloves
½ gal. apple cider
⅔ cup hot cinnamon candies
¼ cup dry orange drink mix
1 qt. water

1. Place cloves in a cheesecloth bag or tea ball.
2. Combine all ingredients in slow cooker.
3. Cover and cook on low 3 to 4 hours.
4. Serve hot from cooker. This cider is especially good during fall or on Halloween.

5 ingredients or less
Hot Mulled Cider

makes 8 servings
ideal slow cooker: 3½-quart

1 tsp. whole cloves
¼ cup brown sugar
2 qts. cider
3-inch cinnamon stick
1 orange, sliced

1. Tie cloves in cheesecloth or put in tea strainer.
2. Combine all ingredients in slow cooker.
3. Cover and cook on low 3 to 6 hours.
4. Remove cloves and serve cider.

Peachy Spiced Cider

makes 8 small servings
ideal slow cooker: 2-quart

4 5½-oz. cans peach nectar
2 cups unsweetened apple juice
½ tsp. ground ginger
¼ tsp. ground cinnamon
¼ tsp. ground nutmeg
4 fresh orange slices, cut ¼-inch
    thick and then halved

1. Combine peach nectar, apple juice, ginger, cinnamon, and nutmeg in slow cooker.
2. Top with orange slices.
3. Cover and cook on low 4 to 6 hours.
4. Remove orange slices and discard; stir before serving.

Wassail

makes 12 servings
ideal slow cooker: 5-quart

2 qts. cider
1 pt. cranberry juice
⅓ to ⅔ cup sugar
1 tsp. aromatic bitters
2 cinnamon sticks
1 tsp. whole allspice
1 small orange, studded with
    whole cloves
1 cup rum (optional)

1. Combine all ingredients in slow cooker. Cover and cook on high 1 hour and then on low 4 to 8 hours.
2. Serve warm from cooker.

note:

• If the wassail turns out to be too sweet for you, add extra cranberry juice until you find a more pleasing flavor balance.

Apple-Honey Tea

makes 6 servings
ideal slow cooker: 3-quart

12-oz. can frozen apple juice or
    cider concentrate
2 Tbsp. instant tea powder
1 Tbsp. honey
½ tsp. ground cinnamon
Apple slices

1. Reconstitute apple juice/cider
concentrate according to package
directions. Pour into slow cooker.
2. Add tea powder, honey, and
cinnamon. Stir to blend.
3. Cover and cook on low 1 to 2
hours.
4. Stir well before serving since
cinnamon tends to settle on bottom. Serve with apple slices.

Fruity Hot Punch

makes 12 servings
ideal slow cooker: 4- or 5-quart

2 16-oz. cans cranberry sauce,
    mashed
4 cups water
1 qt. pineapple juice
¾ cup brown sugar
¼ tsp. salt
¼ tsp. ground nutmeg
¾ tsp. ground cloves
½ tsp. ground allspice
12 cinnamon sticks
Butter (optional)

1. Combine all ingredients except
butter in slow cooker.
2. Cover and cook on low 4 hours.
3. Serve in mugs with cinnamon-
stick stirrers. Dot each serving
with butter, if desired.

Apple-Honey Tea

Almond Tea

makes 12 servings
ideal slow cooker: 5-quart

10 cups boiling water
1 Tbsp. instant tea powder
⅔ cup lemon juice
1 cup sugar
1 tsp. vanilla extract
1 tsp. almond extract

1. Stir together all ingredients in
slow cooker.
2. Cover and cook on high about 1
hour. Turn to low while serving.

Mint Tea

makes 8 servings
ideal slow cooker: 3-quart

2 qts. hot water
Splenda to taste
8 tea bags
2 drops of mint extract

1. Combine water and Splenda
in slow cooker. Mix well until
Splenda dissolves.
2. Add the tea bags and mint
extract.
3. Cover and cook on high 2
hours. Serve hot or cold.

After-Work
Stew

beef and pork

After-Work Stew

makes 5 servings
ideal slow cooker: 3- or
3½-quart oval

3 medium-size red potatoes, pared
  and cubed
4 medium carrots, quartered
2 celery ribs, sliced
2 medium onions, sliced
1½ lbs. beef stew meat, browned
2 tsp. salt
½ tsp. dried basil
½ tsp. pepper
10¾-oz. can tomato soup
Half a soup can of water

1. Layer potatoes, carrots, celery,
and onions in slow cooker.
2. Stir together beef, salt, basil,
and pepper in a bowl and place on
top of vegetables.
3. Combine soup and water. Pour
into slow cooker.
4. Cover and cook on low 6 to 7
hours or until vegetables and meat
are tender.

Beef, Tomatoes, and Noodles

makes 8 servings
ideal slow cooker: 4-quart

1½ lbs. beef stew meat
¼ cup all-purpose flour
2 cups stewed tomatoes (if you like
  tomato chunks) or 2 cups
  crushed tomatoes (if you prefer
  a smoother gravy)
1 tsp. salt
¼ to ½ tsp. pepper
1 medium onion, chopped
Water
12-oz. bag noodles, cooked

1. Stir together meat and flour
until beef is coated. Place in slow
cooker.
2. Add tomatoes, salt, pepper, and
onion. Add water to cover.
3. Cover and cook on high 1 hour
and then on low 4 to 6 hours.
4. Serve over cooked noodles.

Beef Stew

makes 6 servings
ideal slow cooker: 4-quart

2 lbs. beef chuck roast, cubed
¼ to ½ cup all-purpose flour
1½ tsp. salt
½ tsp. pepper
1 tsp. paprika
1 tsp. Worcestershire sauce
1½ cups beef broth
Half of a garlic clove, minced
1 bay leaf
4 carrots, sliced
2 onions, chopped
1 celery rib, sliced
3 potatoes, diced

1. Place meat in slow cooker.
2. Combine flour, salt, pepper,
and paprika. Stir into meat until
coated thoroughly.
3. Stir in remaining ingredients.
4. Cover and cook on high 4 to 6
hours or cook on high 1 hour and
then on low 6 to 10 hours. Remove
bay leaf. Stir stew before serving.

Beef Stew with Shiitake Mushrooms

makes 4 to 6 servings
ideal slow cooker: 4- or 5-quart

12 new potatoes, cut in quarters
½ cup chopped onion
8-oz. pkg. baby carrots
3.4-oz. pkg. fresh shiitake
   mushrooms, sliced, or 2 cups
   regular white mushrooms,
   sliced
16-oz. can whole tomatoes
14-oz. can beef broth
½ cup all-purpose flour
1 Tbsp. Worcestershire sauce
1 tsp. sugar
1 tsp. dried marjoram leaves
¼ tsp. pepper
1 lb. beef stewing meat, trimmed
   of fat and cubed

1. Combine all ingredients except beef in slow cooker. Add beef.
2. Cover and cook on high 1 hour and then on low 6 to 7 hours. Stir well before serving.

Bratwurst Stew

makes 8 servings
ideal slow cooker: 5-quart

2 10¾-oz. cans fat-free chicken
   broth
4 medium carrots, sliced
2 celery ribs, cut in chunks
1 medium onion, chopped
1 tsp. dried basil
½ tsp. garlic powder
3 cups chopped cabbage
2 1-lb. cans great Northern beans,
   drained
5 fully cooked bratwurst links, cut
   in ½-inch slices

1. Combine all ingredients in slow cooker.
2. Cover and cook on high 3 to 4 hours or until veggies are tender.

Bavarian Beef

makes 6 servings
ideal slow cooker: 5-quart

3- to 3½-lb. boneless beef chuck
   roast, cut in half
Oil
3 cups sliced carrot
3 cups sliced onion
2 large kosher dill pickles, chopped
1 cup sliced celery
½ cup dry red wine or beef broth
⅓ cup German-style mustard
2 tsp. coarsely ground black
   pepper
2 bay leaves
¼ tsp. ground cloves
1 cup water
⅓ cup all-purpose flour

1. Brown roast on both sides in oil in skillet. Place in slow cooker.
2. Add remaining ingredients except flour.
3. Cover and cook on low 6 to 7 hours.
4. Remove meat and vegetables to large platter. Cover to keep warm.
5. Mix flour with 1 cup broth until smooth. Return to cooker. Turn slow cooker on high and stir, cooking until broth is smooth and thickened. Remove bay leaves.
6. Serve beef over noodles or spaetzle.

Beef Barbecue Sandwiches

makes 12 to 16 servings
ideal slow cooker: 5-quart

3- to 4-lb. beef roast (bottom
   round or rump is best), cut
   in half
½ cup water
½ cup ketchup
1 tsp. chili powder
1½ Tbsp. Worcestershire sauce
2 Tbsp. cider vinegar
1 tsp. salt
1 Tbsp. sugar
1 tsp. dry mustard
1 medium onion, finely chopped
   (about 1 cup)
½ cup water
12 to 16 Kaiser rolls
Dill pickle slices

1. Place roast in slow cooker; pour ½ cup water into cooker.
2. Cover and cook on high 1 hour and then on low 8 to 10 hours.
3. Meanwhile, combine ketchup and next 8 ingredients and refrigerate 8 to 10 hours.
4. Remove roast from cooker; discard juices. Shred roast with fork and return to cooker. Pour sauce mixture over top. Mix together.
5. Cook on low about 1 hour or until thoroughly heated.
6. Spoon meat mixture into Kaiser rolls using a slotted spoon; spoon additional sauce over top of meat, if desired, and top with pickle slices.

Beef Barbecue Sandwiches

Barbecue Hamburger Steaks

makes 4 servings
ideal slow cooker: 3-quart oval

1 lb. ground chuck

1 tsp. salt

1 tsp. pepper

½ cup milk

1 cup soft bread crumbs (3 slices hearty white bread)

2 Tbsp. brown sugar

2 Tbsp. white vinegar

3 Tbsp. Worcestershire sauce

1 cup ketchup

1. Combine beef, salt, pepper, milk, and bread crumbs. Mix well. Form into 4 patties. Brown patties in large hot skillet and drain.

2. Combine brown sugar, vinegar, Worcestershire sauce, and ketchup in slow cooker. Add ground beef patties.

3. Cover and cook on low 4 hours.

Chicken-Fried Pork Chops

makes 6 servings
ideal slow cooker: 4- or 5-quart

½ cup all-purpose flour

¾ tsp. salt

1½ tsp. dry mustard

¾ tsp. garlic powder

6 pork chops, each cut ¾-inch thick

2 Tbsp. oil

10¾-oz. can cream of chicken soup

1 soup can of water

1. Combine flour, salt, dry mustard, and garlic powder. Dredge pork chops in flour mixture. Brown in oil in skillet. Place in slow cooker.

2. Combine soup and water. Pour over meat.

3. Cover and cook on low 4 to 5 hours or until chops are done.

Casserole Verde

makes 6 servings
ideal slow cooker: 4- or 5-quart

1 lb. ground beef
1 small onion, chopped
⅛ tsp. garlic powder
8-oz. can tomato sauce
⅓ cup chopped black olives
4-oz. can sliced mushrooms
8-oz. container sour cream
8-oz. container cottage cheese
4.25-oz. can chopped green chiles
12-oz. pkg. tortilla chips
2 cups shredded Monterey Jack
   cheese

1. Brown ground beef, onion, and garlic in skillet. Drain. Add tomato sauce, olives, and mushrooms.
2. In a separate bowl, combine sour cream, cottage cheese, and green chiles.
3. In slow cooker, layer a third of the chips, half the ground beef mixture, half the sour cream mixture, and half the shredded cheese. Repeat all layers, except reserve last third of the chips to add just before serving.
4. Cover and cook on low 4 hours.
5. Ten minutes before serving time, scatter reserved chips over top and continue cooking, uncovered.

kid-friendly
Calico Beans

makes 12 to 15 servings
ideal slow cooker: 5- or 6-quart

This is a great dish to serve at neighborhood and family gatherings any time of the year. Kids love it, too.

1 lb. bacon
1 lb. ground beef
½ cup chopped onions
½ cup chopped celery
½ cup ketchup
1 Tbsp. prepared mustard
16-oz. can kidney beans, undrained
16-oz. can great Northern beans,
   undrained
½ cup brown sugar
1 Tbsp. white vinegar
16-oz. can butter beans, undrained
28-oz. can Bush's Baked Beans

1. Cut bacon into small pieces. Brown in skillet. Drain.
2. Brown ground beef in skillet and drain, reserving 2 Tbsp. drippings.
3. Sauté onions and celery in 2 Tbsp. drippings until soft.
4. Combine all ingredients in slow cooker.
5. Cover and cook on low 3 to 4 hours.

Chow Mein

makes 8 servings
ideal slow cooker: 3- or 4-quart

5 boneless pork chops, trimmed of
   fat and cubed
1 to 1½ lbs. round steak, cubed
2 Tbsp. oil
6 cups water
1 celery rib, chopped
1 medium to large onion, chopped
14.5-oz. can bean sprouts, drained
¼ cup low-sodium soy sauce
3 Tbsp. cornstarch (optional)
¼ cup cold water (optional)

1. Brown pork and steak in hot oil in non-stick skillet. Drain.
2. Combine all ingredients except soy sauce, cornstarch, and water in slow cooker.
3. Cover and cook on high 3 to 4 hours.
4. Add soy sauce and thicken with 3 Tbsp. cornstarch mixed with ¼ cup cold water, if desired.
5. Serve over rice or chow mein noodles.

note:

• If your sodium count allows, you may want to add 1 tsp. salt to Step 2.

Cola Roast

makes 8 to 10 servings
ideal slow cooker: 4- or 5-quart

Turn leftovers from this roast into a French dip sandwich using the drippings left in the slow cooker for dipping.

3-lb. beef roast
1.0-oz. envelope dry onion
   soup mix
2 cans cola (do not use diet cola)

1. Place roast in slow cooker. Sprinkle with soup mix. Pour cola over all.
2. Cover and cook on high 1 hour and then on low 5 to 6 hours.

Cooker Chops

makes 4 servings
ideal slow cooker: 3-quart oval

4 pork chops
10¾-oz. can cream of mushroom
   soup
¼ cup ketchup
2 tsp. Worcestershire sauce

1. Place chops in slow cooker.
2. Combine remaining ingredients. Pour over chops.
3. Cover and cook on high 3 to 4 hours or cook on high 1 hour and then on low 6 to 8 hours.

variation:

: • Place thinly sliced onion in
: cooker before adding other
: ingredients.

Corned Beef and Cabbage

makes 12 servings
ideal slow cooker: 4- or 5-quart

3 carrots, cut in 3-inch pieces
2-lb. corned beef brisket, trimmed
   of all fat
2 to 3 medium onions, quartered
¾ to 1¼ cups water
Half a small head of cabbage, cut
   in wedges

1. Layer all ingredients except cabbage in slow cooker.
2. Cover and cook on high 5 to 6 hours or on high 1 hour and then on low 6 to 8 hours.
3. Add cabbage wedges to liquid, pushing down to moisten. Turn to high and cook 2 to 3 hours more.

variations:

: • Add 4 medium potatoes,
: halved, to Step 1.
: • Top individual servings with
: a mixture of sour cream and
: horseradish.

Creamy Ham Topping (for Baked Potatoes)

makes 12 servings
ideal slow cooker: 4-quart

2 Tbsp. butter or margarine
¼ cup all-purpose flour
2 cups fat-free milk
¼ cup fat-free half-and-half
1 Tbsp. chopped parsley
1 Tbsp. sodium-free chicken
   bouillon granules
½ tsp. Italian seasoning
2 cups diced cooked ham
¼ cup grated Romano cheese
1 cup sliced mushrooms

1. Melt butter in saucepan. Stir in flour. Add milk and half-and-half.
2. Stir in remaining ingredients. Pour into slow cooker.
3. Cover and cook on low 1 to 2 hours.
4. Serve over baked potatoes. Top with shredded cheese and sour cream, if desired.

Easy Sweet-and-Sour Pork Chops

makes 6 servings
ideal slow cooker: 5-quart

16-oz. bag frozen Asian vegetables,
   thawed
6 pork chops
12-oz. bottle sweet-and-sour sauce
½ cup water
1 cup frozen pea pods

1. Place vegetables in slow cooker. Arrange chops on top.
2. Combine sauce and water. Pour over chops.
3. Cover and cook on high 1 hour and then on low 5 to 6 hours.
4. Turn to high and add pea pods.
5. Cover and cook on high 5 minutes or until pea pods are crisp-tender.

Flautas with Pork Filling

makes 6 to 8 servings
ideal slow cooker: 4-quart

1 lb. boneless pork roast or chops,
   cubed
1 Tbsp. oil
¼ cup chopped onions
4-oz. can diced green chiles
7-oz. can green chile salsa
1 tsp. cocoa powder
16-oz. can chili

1. Brown cubed pork in hot oil in skillet. Drain. Place pork in slow cooker.
2. Add remaining ingredients except chili.
3. Cover and cook on low 2 to 3 hours.
4. Add chili. Cover and cook 2 to 3 hours longer.
5. Serve on flour tortillas with guacamole dip.

note:

: • This is especially good on spinach-herb tortillas.

Fruited Pork Chops

makes 6 servings
ideal slow cooker: 5- or 6-quart

3 Tbsp. all-purpose flour
1½ tsp. dried oregano
¾ tsp. salt
¼ tsp. garlic powder
¼ tsp. black pepper
6 lean boneless pork loin chops
   (about 5 ozs. each)
1 Tbsp. olive or canola oil
20-oz. can unsweetened pineapple
   chunks
1 cup water
2 Tbsp. brown sugar
2 Tbsp. dried minced onion
2 Tbsp. tomato paste
¼ cup raisins

1. In a large zip-top freezer bag, combine flour, oregano, salt, garlic powder, and pepper.
2. Add pork chops, 1 at a time, and shake to coat.
3. Brown pork chops on both sides in hot oil in a non-stick skillet. Transfer browned chops to slow cooker.

4. Drain pineapple, reserving juice. Set pineapple aside.
5. In a mixing bowl, combine ¾ cup reserved pineapple juice, water, brown sugar, dried onion, and tomato paste. Pour over chops.
6. Sprinkle raisins over top.
7. Cover and cook on high 3 to 3½ hours or until meat is tender and a meat thermometer reads 160°. Stir in reserved pineapple chunks. Cook 10 minutes more or until heated through.

notes:

: • These chops are good served over brown rice.
: • If your diet allows, you may want to use 1 tsp. salt (instead of the ¾ tsp.) in coating mixture in Step 1.

5 ingredients or less

French Dip Roast

makes 8 servings
ideal slow cooker: 4-quart

1 large onion, sliced
3-lb. beef bottom roast, trimmed
   of fat and cut in half
½ cup dry white wine or water
Half a 1-oz. pkg. dry au jus
   gravy mix
2 cups fat-free, low-sodium beef
   broth

1. Place onion in slow cooker. Add roast.
2. Combine wine and gravy mix. Pour over roast.
3. Add enough broth to cover roast.
4. Cover and cook on high 5 to 6 hours or on high 1 hour and then on low 8 to 10 hours.

5. Remove meat from liquid. Let meat stand 5 minutes before slicing thinly across grain.

Garlic Beef Stroganoff

makes 6 to 8 servings
ideal slow cooker: 4- or 5-quart

2 tsp. beef bouillon granules
2 4½-oz. jars sliced mushrooms,
   drained with juice reserved
1 cup mushroom juice, with boiling
   water added to make a full cup
10¾-oz. can cream of mushroom
   soup
1 large onion, chopped
3 garlic cloves, minced
1 Tbsp. Worcestershire sauce
1½- to 2-lb. boneless round steak,
   cut in thin strips
2 Tbsp. oil
8-oz. pkg. cream cheese, cubed
   and softened

1. Dissolve bouillon in mushroom juice and water in slow cooker.
2. Add mushrooms, soup, onion, garlic, and Worcestershire sauce.
3. Sauté beef in oil in skillet. Place in slow cooker and stir into sauce.
4. Cover and cook on low 7 to 8 hours. Turn off heat.
5. Stir in cream cheese until smooth.
6. Serve over noodles.

Good 'n' Easy Beef 'n' Gravy

makes 8 servings
ideal slow cooker: 4- or 5-quart

For the tastiest results, let the rich gravy dribble over mashed potatoes or biscuits.

3-lb. beef roast, cubed
1-oz. envelope dry onion soup mix
½ cup beef broth
10¾-oz. can cream of mushroom or cream of celery soup
4-oz. can sliced mushrooms, drained

1. Combine all ingredients in slow cooker.
2. Cover and cook on high 1 hour and then on low 8 to 10 hours.

variation:

: • Use ½ cup dry white wine
: instead of beef broth.

Ham and Lima Beans

makes 6 servings
ideal slow cooker: 4- or 5-quart

1 lb. dry lima beans
1 onion, chopped
1 bell pepper, chopped
1 tsp. dry mustard
1 tsp. salt
1 tsp. black pepper
½ lb. ham, finely cubed
1 cup water
10¾-oz. can tomato soup

1. Cover beans with water. Soak 8 hours. Drain.
2. Combine all ingredients in slow cooker.

3. Cover and cook on high 4 hours or cook on high 1 hour and then on low 5 hours.
4. If mixture begins to dry out, add ½ cup water or more and stir well.
5. Serve with hot corn bread.

Ground Beef Casserole

makes 8 servings
ideal slow cooker: 6-quart

For a creamier dish, mix half a soup can of water with the mushroom soup before placing over beans.

1½ lbs. lean ground chuck
6 to 8 potatoes, sliced
Water and ½ tsp. cream of tartar
1 medium-size onion, sliced
1 garlic clove, minced
½ tsp. salt
½ tsp. dried basil
½ tsp. dried thyme
¼ tsp. pepper
14½-oz. can cut green beans with juice
10¾-oz. can fat-free, low-sodium cream of mushroom soup

1. Brown the ground chuck in a non-stick skillet; drain and spoon into slow cooker.
2. Slice potatoes into mixing bowl filled with water mixed with cream of tartar to keep potatoes from turning dark. Stir together; then drain potatoes and discard water.
3. Add potatoes, onion, garlic, salt, basil, thyme, and pepper to cooker.
4. Pour beans over all. Spread can of mushroom soup over beans.
5. Cover and cook on low 6 to 8 hours.

Ham and Scalloped Potatoes

makes 8 servings
ideal slow cooker: 6-quart

1½ lbs. 98% fat-free ham, cut in large chunks
9 medium potatoes, peeled and thinly sliced
2 onions, peeled and thinly sliced
½ tsp. salt
¼ tsp. pepper or to taste
1 cup fat-free shredded Cheddar or American cheese
10¾-oz. can 98% fat-free cream of celery soup
Paprika

1. Layer half each of ham, potatoes, and onion in slow cooker. Sprinkle with half each of salt and pepper and then half of grated cheese. Repeat layers.
2. Spoon soup over ingredients.
3. Cover and cook on high 4 hours or on high 1 hour and then on low 6 to 8 hours. Sprinkle with paprika.

Ham and Scalloped
Potatoes

1. Brown roast on all sides in oil in skillet. Place in slow cooker. Add remaining ingredients.

2. Cover and cook on low 8 to 10 hours.

kid-friendly

Hungarian Goulash

makes 10 servings
ideal slow cooker: 4-quart

1 lb. extra-lean ground beef
1 large onion, sliced
1 garlic clove, minced
½ cup ketchup
2 Tbsp. Worcestershire sauce
1 Tbsp. brown sugar
1 to 1½ tsp. salt
2 tsp. paprika
½ tsp. dry mustard
1 cup water
¼ cup all-purpose flour
¼ cup cold water

1. Place meat in slow cooker. Cover with onion.

2. Combine garlic, ketchup, Worcestershire sauce, sugar, salt, paprika, mustard, and 1 cup water. Pour over meat.

3. Cover and cook on high 1 hour and then on low 3 to 4 hours.

4. Dissolve flour in ¼ cup cold water. Stir into meat mixture.

5. Cover and cook on high 10 to 15 minutes or until slightly thickened.

6. Serve over noodles or rice.

Hamburger-Green Bean Dish

makes 4 to 5 servings
ideal slow cooker: 4- or 5-quart

1 lb. ground beef
1 onion, chopped
1 qt. string beans, cut into 1½-inch pieces
10¾-oz. can tomato soup
¾ tsp. salt
¼ tsp. pepper
6 to 7 cups mashed potatoes
1 egg, beaten

1. Brown meat and onion in skillet. Stir in beans, soup, salt, and pepper. Pour into slow cooker.

2. Combine mashed potatoes and egg. Spread over meat mixture in slow cooker.

3. Cover and cook on low 5 to 6 hours or until beans are tender.

Horseradish Beef

makes 6 to 8 servings
ideal slow cooker: 4-quart

3-lb. pot roast, trimmed of fat and cut in half
1 Tbsp. canola oil
½ tsp. salt
½ tsp. pepper
1 medium onion, chopped
6-oz. can tomato paste
¼ cup horseradish sauce

beef and pork 97

Jean & Tammy's Sloppy Joes

makes 14 servings
ideal slow cooker: 4-quart

2¾ lbs. 85%-lean ground beef, browned, drained, and patted dry
1 onion, finely chopped
1 green bell pepper, chopped
8-oz. can tomato sauce
8-oz. can no-salt-added tomato sauce
¾ cup ketchup
1 Tbsp. Worcestershire sauce
1 tsp. chili powder
¼ tsp. black pepper
¼ tsp. garlic powder
Sandwich rolls

1. Combine all ingredients except rolls in slow cooker.
2. Cover and cook on high 3 to 4 hours or on high 1 hour and then on low 6 to 8 hours.
3. Serve in sandwich rolls.

Meat Loaf and Mushrooms

makes 6 servings
ideal slow cooker: 3½- or 4-quart

2 1-oz. slices whole wheat bread
½ lb. extra-lean ground beef
¾ lb. fat-free ground turkey
1½ cups sliced mushrooms
½ cup minced onion
1 tsp. Italian seasoning
¾ tsp. salt
2 eggs
1 garlic clove, minced
3 Tbsp. ketchup
1½ tsp. Dijon mustard
⅛ tsp. ground red pepper

1. Fold 2 strips of aluminum foil—each long enough to fit from the top of the cooker, down inside, and up the other side, plus a 2-inch overhang on each side of the cooker—to function as handles for lifting the finished loaf out of the cooker.
2. Process bread slices in food processor until crumbs measure 1⅓ cups.
3. Combine bread crumbs, beef, turkey, mushrooms, onion, Italian seasoning, salt, eggs, and garlic in bowl. Shape into loaf to fit in slow cooker.
4. Mix together ketchup, mustard, and pepper. Spread over top of loaf.
5. Cover and cook on high 1 hour and then on low 3 hours.
6. When finished, pull up loaf gently with foil handles. Place loaf on warm platter. Pull foil handles away. Allow loaf to rest for 10 minutes before slicing.

Meat Loaf Sensation

makes 8 servings
ideal slow cooker: 4- or 5-quart oval

2½ lbs. ground chuck
1 cup salsa
1.25-oz. pkg. dry taco seasoning
2 eggs, slightly beaten
1 cup dry bread crumbs
3 cups shredded Mexican four-cheese blend
½ tsp. salt
½ tsp. pepper

1. Combine all ingredients and mix well. Shape into loaf and place in lightly greased slow cooker.
2. Cover and cook on high 1 hour and then on low 3 hours.

Pork Chops on Rice

makes 4 servings
ideal slow cooker: 4- or 5-quart

½ cup uncooked brown rice
⅔ cup uncooked converted white rice
¼ cup butter or margarine
½ cup chopped onions
4-oz. can sliced mushrooms, drained
½ tsp. dried thyme
½ tsp. ground sage
½ tsp. salt
¼ tsp. pepper
4 boneless pork chops, ¾-inch to 1-inch thick
10½-oz. can beef consommé
2 Tbsp. Worcestershire sauce
½ tsp. dried thyme
½ tsp. paprika
¼ tsp. ground nutmeg

1. Sauté brown and white rice in butter in skillet until rice is golden.
2. Remove from heat and stir in onions, mushrooms, thyme, sage, salt, and pepper. Pour into greased slow cooker.
3. Arrange chops over rice.
4. Combine consommé and Worcestershire sauce. Pour over chops.
5. Combine thyme, paprika, and nutmeg. Sprinkle over chops.
6. Cover and cook on high 4 to 5 hours or cook on high 1 hour and then on low 5 to 7 hours.

Pot Roast

makes 8 servings
ideal slow cooker: 5-quart

4 medium potatoes, cubed
4 carrots, sliced
1 onion, sliced
3 to 4-lb. rump roast, or pot roast, cut into serving-size pieces
1 tsp. salt
½ tsp. pepper
1 beef bouillon cube
½ cup boiling water

1. Place vegetables and meat in slow cooker. Stir in salt and pepper.
2. Dissolve bouillon cube in boiling water. Pour over all.
3. Cover and cook on high 1 hour; reduce heat to low and cook 8 to 10 hours.

Powerhouse Beef Roast with Tomatoes, Onions, and Peppers

makes 5 to 6 servings
ideal slow cooker: 4- or 5-quart

3-lb. boneless chuck roast, trimmed of fat and cut in half
1 garlic clove, minced
1 Tbsp. canola oil
2 to 3 medium onions, sliced
2 to 3 green and red bell peppers, sliced
16-oz. jar salsa
2 14½-oz. cans Mexican-style stewed tomatoes

1. Brown roast and garlic in oil in skillet. Place in slow cooker.
2. Add onions and bell peppers.
3. Combine salsa and tomatoes and pour over ingredients into slow cooker.

4. Cover and cook on low 8 to 10 hours.
5. Slice meat to serve.

note:

• Make Beef Burritos with the leftovers. Shred the beef and heat with remaining bell peppers, onions, and ½ cup broth. Add 1 Tbsp. chili powder, 2 tsp. cumin, and salt to taste. Heat thoroughly. Fill warm flour tortillas with mixture and serve with sour cream, salsa, and guacamole.

Old-World Sauerbraten

makes 12 servings
ideal slow cooker: 5-quart

4-lb. lean beef rump roast, cut in half
1 cup water
1 cup vinegar
1 lemon, unpeeled, sliced
10 whole cloves
1 large onion, sliced
4 bay leaves
5 whole peppercorns
2 Tbsp. salt
2 Tbsp. sugar
12 low-fat gingersnaps, crumbled

1. Place meat in deep ceramic or glass bowl.
2. Combine water, vinegar, lemon, cloves, onion, bay leaves, peppercorns, salt, and sugar. Pour over meat. Cover and refrigerate 24 to 36 hours. Turn meat several times while marinating.
3. Place beef in slow cooker. Pour 1 cup marinade over meat.
4. Cover and cook on high 1 hour and then on low 4 to 6 hours. Remove meat.

5. Strain meat juices and return liquid to pot. Turn to high. Stir in gingersnaps. Cover and cook on high 10 to 14 minutes.
6. Allow meat to rest 15 minutes. Slice. Then pour finished sauce over meat to serve.

Quick Lasagna

makes 6 servings
ideal slow cooker: 4-quart

¼ lb. extra-lean ground beef
8-oz. pkg. broad egg noodles
1 cup fat-free cottage cheese
½ cup shredded low-fat mozzarella cheese
¼ cup grated Parmesan cheese
2½ cups spaghetti sauce

1. Brown ground beef in a non-stick skillet. Set aside.
2. Cook noodles and drain. Toss noodles with cheeses.
3. Mix together browned beef and spaghetti sauce.
4. Spoon one-third of meat sauce in slow cooker.
5. Layer half of noodles. Repeat layers.
6. Cover and cook on low 5 to 6 hours.

note:

• If you wish, add 1 Tbsp. Italian seasoning or 1½ tsp. dried basil and 1½ tsp. dried oregano to Step 3.

Pork Chops with Stuffing

makes 2 servings
ideal slow cooker: 3- or 4-quart

4 slices bread, cubed
1 egg
¼ cup grated or finely chopped
   celery
¼ to ½ tsp. salt
⅛ tsp. pepper
2 thickly cut pork chops
1 cup water

1. Combine bread cubes, egg, celery, salt, and pepper.
2. Cut pork chops partway through, creating pockets. Fill with stuffing.
3. Pour water into slow cooker. Add chops.
4. Cover and cook on high 1 hour and then on low 2 to 3 hours.

"Smothered" Steak

makes 6 servings
ideal slow cooker: 4-quart

1½-lb. chuck or round steak,
   trimmed of fat and cut in strips
⅓ cup all-purpose flour
¼ tsp. black pepper
1 large onion, sliced
1 green bell pepper, sliced
14½-oz. can stewed tomatoes
4-oz. can mushrooms, drained
2 Tbsp. soy sauce
10-oz. pkg. frozen French-style
   green beans

1. Layer steak in slow cooker. Sprinkle with flour and pepper. Stir well to coat steak.
2. Add remaining ingredients. Mix together gently.

3. Cover and cook on high 1 hour and then on low 6 hours.
4. Serve over rice.

Savory Pork Roast

makes 8 to 10 servings
ideal slow cooker: 4-quart

3-lb. boneless pork loin roast,
   trimmed of fat
1 large onion, sliced
1 bay leaf
2 Tbsp. soy sauce
1 Tbsp. garlic powder

1. Place roast and onion in slow cooker. Add bay leaf, soy sauce, and garlic powder.
2. Cover and cook on high 1 hour and then on low 6 hours.
3. Remove bay leaf. Slice roast and serve.

Spaghetti Sauce with a Kick

makes 4 to 6 servings
ideal slow cooker: 4-quart

1 lb. ground beef
1 onion, chopped
2 28-oz. cans crushed tomatoes
16-oz. can tomato sauce
1 lb. Italian sausage, cut in chunks
3 garlic cloves, crushed
1 Tbsp. Italian seasoning
2 tsp. dried basil
Red pepper flakes to taste

1. Brown beef and onion in skillet. Drain and place in slow cooker.
2. Add remaining ingredients.
3. Cover and cook on low 4 to 6 hours.
4. Serve over your favorite pasta.

note:

• Add 1 to 2 tsp. salt and 1 to 2 Tbsp. brown sugar or honey to Step 2, if desired.

Shepherd's Pie

makes 3 to 4 servings
ideal slow cooker: 3- or 4-quart

1 lb. ground pork
1 Tbsp. vinegar
1 tsp. salt
¼ tsp. hot pepper
1 tsp. paprika
¼ tsp. dried oregano
¼ tsp. black pepper
1 tsp. chili powder
1 small onion, chopped
15-oz. can corn, drained
3 large potatoes
¼ cup milk
1 tsp. butter
¼ tsp. salt
Dash of pepper
Shredded Cheddar cheese

1. Combine pork, vinegar, and seasonings. Cook in skillet until brown. Add onion and cook until onion begins to glaze. Spread in bottom of slow cooker.
2. Spread corn over meat.
3. Boil potatoes until soft. Mash with milk, butter, ¼ tsp. salt, and dash of pepper. Spread over meat and corn.
4. Cover and cook on low 3 hours. Sprinkle top with cheese a few minutes before serving.

Shepherd's Pie

Stuffed Green Bell Peppers

makes 6 servings
ideal slow cooker: 5-quart

6 green bell peppers
1 lb. ground beef
¼ cup chopped onion
1 tsp. salt
¼ tsp. black pepper
1¼ cups cooked rice
1 Tbsp. Worcestershire sauce
8-oz. can tomato sauce
¼ cup beef broth

1. Cut stem ends from bell peppers. Carefully remove seeds and membrane without breaking pepper apart. Parboil in water 5 minutes. Drain. Set aside.
2. Brown ground beef and onion in skillet. Drain off drippings. Place meat and onion in mixing bowl.
3. Add seasonings, rice, and Worcestershire sauce to meat and combine well. Stuff bell peppers with mixture. Stand stuffed bell peppers upright in slow cooker.

4. Mix together tomato sauce and beef broth. Pour over peppers.
5. Cover and cook on low 5 to 7 hours.

Herb Potato-Fish Bake

seafood

Herb Potato-Fish Bake

makes 4 servings
ideal slow cooker: 3½-quart oval

10¾-oz. can cream of celery soup
½ cup water
4 fresh or thawed frozen orange
    roughy fillets (1½ lbs.)
2 cups cooked, diced red potatoes,
    drained (6 small potatoes
    quartered)
¼ cup grated fresh Parmesan
    cheese
1 Tbsp. chopped fresh parsley
½ tsp. dried basil
¼ tsp. dried oregano
Lemon wedges (optional)

1. Combine soup and water. Pour
half in slow cooker. Arrange fillets
on top. Place potatoes on fillets.
Pour remaining soup mixture
over top.
2. Combine cheese and herbs.
Sprinkle over ingredients in slow
cooker.

3. Cover and cook on high 1 to 2
hours, being careful not to over-
cook fish.
4. Serve with lemon wedges, if
desired.

Tex-Mex Luau

makes 6 servings
ideal slow cooker: 3- or 4-quart

1½ lbs. frozen firm-textured fish
    fillets, thawed
2 onions, thinly sliced
2 lemons, divided
2 Tbsp. butter, melted
2 tsp. salt
1 bay leaf
4 whole peppercorns
1 cup water
Avocado Sauce

1. Cut fillets into serving portions.
2. Combine onion and 1 sliced
lemon in butter, along with salt,
bay leaf, and peppercorns. Pour
into slow cooker.

3. Place fillets on top of onion and
lemon slices. Add water.
4. Cover and cook on high 3 to 4
hours.
5. Before serving, carefully remove
fish fillets with slotted spoon.
Place on heatproof plate.
6. Sprinkle with juice of half of the
second lemon. Slice remaining half
of lemon for garnish.
7. Serve hot with Avocado Sauce,
if desired. Or chill and serve cold
with Avocado Sauce, if you wish.

avocado sauce

makes 1½ cups

7½ ozs. frozen low-fat avocado dip,
    thawed
½ cup fat-free sour cream
2 Tbsp. lemon juice
Half a small onion, finely chopped

1. Combine all ingredients. Mix
well.

Company Seafood Pasta

makes 4 to 6 servings
ideal slow cooker: 3-quart

. . . .

2 cups sour cream

3 cups shredded Monterey Jack
    cheese

2 Tbsp. butter or margarine,
    melted

½ lb. crabmeat or imitation flaked
    crabmeat

⅛ tsp. pepper

½ lb. bay scallops, lightly cooked

1 lb. medium-size fresh shrimp,
    cooked and peeled

Chopped fresh parsley

1. Combine sour cream, cheese,
and butter in slow cooker.

2. Stir in remaining ingredients
except parsley.
3. Cover and cook on low 1 to 2
hours.
4. Serve immediately over lin-
guine. Garnish with fresh parsley.

5 ingredients or less

Curried Shrimp

makes 5 servings
ideal slow cooker: 3- or 4-quart

. . . .

1 small onion, chopped

2 cups cooked peeled shrimp

1 tsp. curry powder

10¾-oz. can 98% fat-free, lower-
    sodium cream of mushroom
    soup

1 cup fat-free sour cream

1. Combine all ingredients except
sour cream in slow cooker.

2. Cover and cook on low 4 to 6
hours.

3. Ten minutes before serving, stir
in sour cream.

4. Serve over rice or puff pastry.

5 ingredients or less

Oyster Stew

makes 8 servings
ideal slow cooker: 3-quart

. . . .

2 qts. 2% reduced-fat milk

3 Tbsp. butter

2 pints fresh oysters

1½ tsp. salt

2 tsp. Worcestershire sauce

1. Heat milk in covered slow cooker on high 1½ hours.
2. In a saucepan, melt butter. Add oysters with liquid. Simmer on low until edges of oysters curl.
3. Add salt and Worcestershire sauce to oysters. Pour into slow cooker.
4. Cover and cook on low 2 to 3 hours, stirring occasionally.

Company Casserole

makes 4 to 6 servings
ideal slow cooker: 4- or 5-quart

1¼ cups uncooked converted rice
½ cup butter, melted
3 cups chicken broth
3 to 4 cups diced cooked chicken breasts
2 4-oz. cans sliced mushrooms, drained
⅓ cup soy sauce
12-oz. pkg. shelled frozen raw shrimp
⅔ cup slivered almonds
8 green onions, chopped, 2 Tbsp. reserved

1. Combine rice and butter in slow cooker. Stir to coat rice well.
2. Add remaining ingredients except almonds and 2 Tbsp. green onions.
3. Cover and cook on high 3 to 4 hours or on low 6 to 8 hours until rice is tender.
4. Sprinkle almonds and 2 Tbsp. green onions over top before serving.
5. Serve with green beans, tossed salad, and fruit.

kid-friendly
Tuna Barbecue

makes 4 servings
ideal slow cooker: 3- or 4-quart

12-oz. can tuna, packed in water, drained
2 cups no-salt-added tomato juice
1 medium-size green bell pepper, finely chopped
2 Tbsp. onion flakes
2 Tbsp. Worcestershire sauce
3 Tbsp. vinegar
2 Tbsp. sugar
1 Tbsp. prepared mustard
1 celery rib, chopped
Dash of chili powder
½ tsp. cinnamon
Dash of hot sauce (optional)
Sandwich buns

1. Combine all ingredients except buns in slow cooker.
2. Cover and cook on high 4 to 5 hours or on low 8 to 10 hours. If mixture becomes too dry while cooking, add ½ cup tomato juice.
3. Serve on buns.

Clam Chowder

makes 8 to 12 servings
ideal slow cooker: 4-quart

2 10¾-oz. cans cream of potato soup
10¾-oz. can cream of celery soup
2 6½-oz. cans minced clams, drained
3 bacon slices, diced and cooked
1 soup can of water
1 small onion, minced
1 Tbsp. chopped fresh parsley
Dash of dried marjoram
1 Tbsp. Worcestershire sauce
Pepper to taste
2 soup cans of milk

1. Combine all ingredients except milk in slow cooker.
2. Cover and cook on low 6 to 8 hours. Twenty minutes before end of cooking time, stir in milk. Continue cooking until heated through.

Corn and Shrimp Chowder

makes 6 servings
ideal slow cooker: 3- or 4-quart

4 bacon slices, diced
1 cup chopped onions
2 cups diced, unpeeled red potatoes
2 10-oz. pkgs. frozen corn kernels
1 tsp. Worcestershire sauce
½ tsp. paprika
½ tsp. salt
⅛ tsp. pepper
2 6-oz. cans shrimp
2 cups water
2 Tbsp. butter or margarine
12-oz. can evaporated milk
Chopped fresh chives

1. Cook bacon in skillet until lightly crisp. Add onions to drippings and sauté until transparent. Using slotted spoon, transfer bacon and onions to slow cooker.
2. Add remaining ingredients except milk and chives to cooker.
3. Cover and cook on low 3 to 4 hours, adding milk and chives last 30 minutes of cooking.
4. Serve with broccoli salad.

Crab Soup

makes 10 servings
ideal slow cooker: 5-quart

1 lb. carrots, sliced
½ bunch celery, sliced
1 large onion, diced
2 10-oz. bags frozen mixed
    vegetables or your choice of
    frozen vegetables
12-oz. can no-added-salt tomato
    juice
8 ozs. extra-lean, lower-sodium ham
1 lb. beef, cubed
6 slices bacon, chopped
¼ tsp. pepper
1 Tbsp. Old Bay seasoning
1 lb. claw crabmeat

1. Combine all ingredients except
seasonings and crabmeat in slow
cooker. Pour in water until cooker
is half full.
2. Add seasonings. Stir thoroughly.
Place crabmeat on top.
3. Cover and cook on low 8 to 10
hours.
4. Stir well and serve.

Shrimp Marinara

makes 6 servings
ideal slow cooker: 3½-quart

16-oz. can low-sodium tomatoes,
    cut up
2 Tbsp. minced parsley
1 garlic clove, minced
½ tsp. dried basil
½ tsp. salt
¼ tsp. black pepper
1 tsp. dried oregano
6-oz. can tomato paste
½ tsp. seasoned salt
1 lb. shrimp, cooked and peeled
3 cups hot cooked spaghetti
Grated Parmesan cheese

1. Combine tomatoes, parsley,
garlic, basil, salt, pepper, oregano,
tomato paste, and seasoned salt in
slow cooker.
2. Cover and cook on low 6 to 7
hours.
3. Stir shrimp into sauce.
4. Cover and cook on high 10 to
15 minutes.
5. Serve over hot cooked spaghetti.
Top with Parmesan cheese.

Chicken and Seafood Gumbo

makes 12 servings
ideal slow cooker: 5- or 6-quart

1 cup chopped celery
1 cup chopped onions
½ cup chopped green bell
    pepper
¼ cup olive oil
¼ cup plus 1 Tbsp. all-purpose
    flour
6 cups 100%-fat-free, 30-50%
    lower-sodium chicken broth
2 lbs. chicken, cut up and trimmed
    of skin and fat
3 bay leaves
1½ cups sliced okra
14½-oz. can diced tomatoes
1 tsp. Tabasco sauce
Salt to taste
Black pepper to taste
1 lb. ready-to-eat shrimp
½ cup snipped fresh parsley

1. Sauté celery, onions, and green
pepper in oil. Blend in flour and
chicken broth until smooth. Cook
5 minutes or until mixture begins
to thicken, stirring constantly.
Pour into slow cooker.
2. Add remaining ingredients
except shrimp and parsley.

3. Cover and cook on low 9 to
11 hours or until chicken and
vegetables are done.
4. Add shrimp and parsley and
cook on low 1 more hour.
5. Remove bay leaves before serving.
6. Serve with white rice.

Shrimp Jambalaya

makes 8 servings
ideal slow cooker: 5-quart

2 Tbsp. margarine
2 medium onions, chopped
2 green bell peppers, chopped
3 celery ribs, chopped
1 cup chopped cooked lean ham
2 garlic cloves, chopped
1½ cups uncooked instant rice
1½ cups fat-free, low-sodium beef
    broth
28-oz. can low-sodium chopped
    tomatoes
2 Tbsp. chopped parsley, fresh or
    dried
1 tsp. dried basil
½ tsp. dried thyme
¼ tsp. black pepper
⅛ tsp. cayenne pepper
1 lb. peeled, deveined, medium-
    size shrimp
1 Tbsp. chopped parsley

1. Half an hour before assembling
recipe, melt margarine on high
in slow cooker. Add onion, green
pepper, celery, ham, and garlic.
Cook 30 minutes.
2. Add rice. Cover and cook 15
minutes.
3. Add broth, tomatoes, 2 Tbsp.
parsley, and remaining seasonings.
Cover and cook on high 1 hour.
4. Add shrimp. Cook 30 minutes
more or until liquid is absorbed.
5. Garnish with 1 Tbsp. parsley.

Shrimp Jambalaya

Melanie's Chicken
Cordon Bleu (page 112)

poultry

Another Chicken in a Pot

makes 4 to 6 servings
ideal slow cooker: 4- or 5-quart

1 lb. bag baby carrots

1 small onion, diced

10-oz. pkg. frozen green beans, thawed

3-lb. whole chicken, cut in serving-size pieces, skin and fat removed

½ tsp. salt

½ tsp. black pepper

½ cup chicken broth

¼ cup dry white wine

½ to 1 tsp. dried basil

1. Put carrots, onion, and beans in slow cooker. Add chicken. Top with salt, pepper, broth, and wine. Sprinkle with basil.

2. Cover and cook on high 3½ to 5 hours or on high 1 hour and then on low 1½ to 3 hours.

Chicken Casablanca

makes 6 to 8 servings
ideal slow cooker: 4- or 5-quart

2 large onions, sliced

1 tsp. ground ginger

3 garlic cloves, minced

2 Tbsp. canola oil

3 large carrots, diced

2 large potatoes, unpeeled, diced

3 lbs. skinless chicken pieces

½ tsp. ground cumin

½ tsp. salt

½ tsp. pepper

¼ tsp. cinnamon

2 Tbsp. raisins

14½-oz. can chopped tomatoes

3 small zucchini, sliced

15-oz. can garbanzo beans, drained

2 Tbsp. chopped fresh parsley

1. Sauté onion, ginger, and garlic in oil in skillet. Place onion mixture in slow cooker, reserving oil. Sauté carrots and potatoes in oil. Place in slow cooker, reserving oil.

2. Brown chicken over medium heat in reserved oil. Place in slow cooker. Mix gently with vegetables.

3. Combine seasonings in separate bowl. Sprinkle over chicken and vegetables. Add raisins and tomatoes.

4. Cover and cook on high 4 to 6 hours.

5. Add sliced zucchini, beans, and parsley 30 minutes before serving.

6. Serve over cooked rice or couscous.

variation:

• Add ½ tsp. turmeric and ¼ tsp. cayenne pepper to Step 3.

Sunday Roast Chicken

makes 4 or 5 servings
ideal slow cooker: 5- or 6-quart

Seasoning Mix:
1 Tbsp. salt
2 tsp. paprika
1½ tsp. onion powder
1½ tsp. garlic powder
1½ tsp. dried basil
1 tsp. dry mustard
1 tsp. cumin
2 tsp. black pepper
½ tsp. dried thyme
½ tsp. savory
Chicken:
2 Tbsp. butter
2 cups chopped onion
1 cup chopped green bell pepper
1 roasting chicken, cut in half
¼ cup all-purpose flour
1 to 2 cups chicken stock

1. Combine seasoning mix ingredients in small bowl.
2. Melt butter over high heat in skillet. When butter starts to sizzle, add onion, green pepper, and 3 Tbsp. seasoning mix. Cook until onion is golden brown. Cool.
3. Stuff cavity of chicken with cooled vegetables.
4. Sprinkle outside of chicken with 1 Tbsp. seasoning mix. Rub in well.
5. Place chicken in slow cooker.
6. Cover and cook on high 1 hour and then on low 4 hours.
7. Empty vegetable stuffing and juices into saucepan. Whisk in flour and 1 cup stock. Cook over high heat until thickened. Add more stock if you prefer a thinner gravy.

Greek Chicken

makes 4 to 6 servings
ideal slow cooker: 4-quart

4 potatoes, unpeeled, quartered
2 lbs. chicken pieces, trimmed of skin and fat
2 large onions, quartered
1 whole garlic bulb, minced
3 tsp. dried oregano
¾ tsp. salt
½ tsp. pepper
1 Tbsp. olive oil

1. Place potatoes in slow cooker. Add chicken, onion, and garlic. Sprinkle with seasonings. Top with oil.
2. Cover and cook on high 5 to 6 hours or on high 1 hour and then on low 7 to 8 hours.

5 ingredients or less

Chicken Rice Dish

makes 4 servings
ideal slow cooker: 4-quart

1 cup cooked rice
10¾-oz. can cream of chicken soup
1 cup chicken broth
4 chicken thighs, browned
10-oz. pkg. frozen broccoli, thawed

1. Combine rice, soup, chicken broth, and chicken thighs. Place mixture in slow cooker.
2. Cover and cook on low 3½ hours.
3. Stir in broccoli and cook on low 30 minutes.

Dad's Spicy Chicken Curry

makes 8 servings
ideal slow cooker: 5- or 6-quart

4 lbs. chicken pieces, with bones
2 onions, diced
10-oz. pkg. frozen chopped spinach, thawed and squeezed dry
1 cup plain yogurt
2 to 3 red potatoes, diced
3 tsp. salt
1 tsp. garlic powder
1 tsp. ground ginger
1 tsp. ground cumin
1 tsp. ground coriander
1 tsp. black pepper
1 tsp. ground cloves
1 tsp. ground cardamom
1 tsp. ground cinnamon
½ tsp. chili powder
1 tsp. red bell pepper flakes
3 tsp. turmeric

1. Place chicken in slow cooker. Cover with water.
2. Cover and cook on high 2 hours or until tender.
3. Drain chicken. Remove from slow cooker. Cool briefly and cut or shred in small pieces. Return to slow cooker.
4. Add remaining ingredients.
5. Cover and cook on low 4 to 6 hours or until potatoes are tender.
6. Serve over rice. Accompany with fresh mango slices or mango chutney.

variation:

• Substitute 5 tsp. curry powder for the garlic powder, ginger, cumin, coriander, and black pepper.

Levi's Sesame Chicken Wings

makes 6 to 8 servings
ideal slow cooker: 4-quart

3 lbs. chicken wings
Salt to taste
Pepper to taste
1¾ cups honey
1 cup soy sauce
½ cup ketchup
2 Tbsp. canola oil
2 Tbsp. sesame oil
2 garlic cloves, minced
Toasted sesame seeds

1. Rinse wings. Cut at joint.
Sprinkle with salt and pepper.
Place on broiler pan.
2. Broil 5 inches from top, 10 minutes on each side. Place chicken in
slow cooker.
3. Combine remaining ingredients
except sesame seeds. Pour mixture
over chicken.
4. Cover and cook on high
2½ hours or on low 5 hours.
5. Sprinkle sesame seeds over top
just before serving.
6. Serve as appetizer or as a meal
with white or brown rice and
shredded lettuce.

**Levi's Sesame
Chicken Wings**

15-minute prep

Sweet Aromatic Chicken

makes 4 servings
ideal slow cooker: 4-quart

½ cup coconut milk
½ cup water
8 chicken thighs, skinned
½ cup brown sugar
2 Tbsp. soy sauce
⅛ tsp. ground cloves
2 garlic cloves, minced

1. Combine coconut milk and
water. Pour into greased slow
cooker.
2. Add remaining ingredients in
order listed.
3. Cover and cook on high 1 hour
and then on low 3 to 4 hours.

leftover coconut milk?

• Two or three spoonfuls over
vanilla ice cream makes a quick
and flavorful dessert.
• Family piña coladas are also
good. Pour the coconut milk into
a pitcher; add one large can pineapple juice. Serve over ice.

5 ingredients or less

Chicken in Wine

makes 4 to 6 servings
ideal slow cooker: 4-quart

2 lbs. chicken breasts or pieces,
    trimmed of skin and fat
10¾-oz. can 98% fat-free, reduced-
    sodium cream of mushroom soup
10¾-oz. can French onion soup
1 cup dry white wine or chicken
    broth

1. Place chicken in slow cooker.
2. Combine soups and wine. Pour
over chicken.
3. Cover and cook on high 1 hour
and then on low 4 to 6 hours.
4. Serve over rice, pasta, or
potatoes.

Fruited Barbecue Chicken

makes 4 to 6 servings
ideal slow cooker: 4- or 5-quart

28-oz. can tomato sauce
20-oz. can unsweetened crushed
  pineapple, undrained
2 Tbsp. brown sugar
3 Tbsp. white vinegar
1 Tbsp. instant minced onion
1 tsp. paprika
2 tsp. Worcestershire sauce
¼ tsp. garlic powder
⅛ tsp. pepper
3 lbs. skinned chicken thighs
11-oz. can mandarin oranges,
  drained

1. Combine all ingredients except chicken and oranges in slow cooker. Add chicken pieces.
2. Cover and cook on high 4 hours.
3. Just before serving, stir in oranges. Serve over rice.

5 ingredients or less

Mushroom Chicken

makes 4 servings
ideal slow cooker: 4-quart

1 lb. boneless, skinless chicken
  breast halves
4.5-oz. pkg. dry chicken gravy mix
10¾-oz. can cream of mushroom
  or chicken soup
1 cup dry white wine
8-oz. pkg. cream cheese, softened

1. Place chicken in slow cooker. Sprinkle gravy mix over chicken. In a bowl, combine soup and wine and pour over gravy mix.

2. Cover and cook on high 1 hour and then on low 5½ hours. Stir in cream cheese and cook on low 30 minutes.
3. Before serving, remove chicken (keeping it warm) and whisk sauce until smooth.
4. Serve chicken and sauce over noodles or rice.

for the holidays

Melanie's Chicken Cordon Bleu

makes 6 servings
ideal slow cooker: 4-quart

pictured on page 108

6 large boneless, skinless chicken
  breast halves
6 pieces thinly sliced ham (½ oz.
  per slice)
6 thin slices reduced-fat Swiss
  cheese (½ oz. per slice)
Salt to taste
Pepper to taste
6 slices bacon, gently browned
  but not crispy, drained, and
  patted dry
¼ cup water
1 tsp. salt-free chicken bouillon
  powder
½ cup white cooking wine
1 tsp. cornstarch
¼ cup cold water

1. Flatten chicken to ⅛- to ¼-inch thickness. Place a slice of ham and a slice of cheese on top of each flattened breast. Sprinkle with salt and pepper. Roll up and wrap with strip of bacon. Secure with toothpick. Place in slow cooker.
2. Combine ¼ cup water, bouillon powder, and wine. Pour into slow cooker.

3. Cover and cook on high 4 hours.
4. Combine cornstarch and ¼ cup cold water. Add to slow cooker. Cook until sauce thickens.

kid-friendly

Parmesan Chicken

makes 8 servings
ideal slow cooker: 4- or 5-quart

8 boneless, skinless chicken breast
  halves (about 2 lbs.)
½ cup water
1 cup fat-free mayonnaise
½ cup grated fat-free Parmesan
  cheese
2 tsp. dried oregano
¼ tsp. black pepper
¼ tsp. paprika

1. Place chicken and water in slow cooker.
2. Cover and cook on high 2 hours.
3. Mix remaining 5 ingredients. Spread over chicken.
4. Cover and cook on high 2 to 2½ hours.

Apricot-Mustard Chicken

makes 6 servings
ideal slow cooker: 5- or 6-quart

11½-oz. can apricot nectar
2 Tbsp. Dijon mustard
1 garlic clove, minced
¼ tsp. grated fresh ginger
¼ tsp. cayenne pepper
¼ tsp. ground allspice
¼ tsp. turmeric
¼ tsp. ground cardamom
6 boneless, skinless chicken breast
  halves
4 cups cooked couscous or wild rice
  (blended is good, too)

1. Combine all ingredients except chicken and couscous in slow cooker; stir gently.
2. Add chicken, turning to make sure all sides are covered in sauce.
3. Cover and cook on high 2½ to 3 hours or on high 1 hour and then on low 3 to 4 hours.
4. Remove chicken and arrange over warm couscous or rice. Pour the sauce over the chicken and serve.

Chicken and Sun-Dried Tomatoes

makes 8 servings
ideal slow cooker: 6-quart

1 Tbsp. olive oil
8 (about 3 lbs.) boneless, skinless chicken breast halves
2 garlic cloves, minced
½ cup dry white wine
1½ cups fat-free, low-sodium chicken broth
1 tsp. dried basil
½ cup chopped sun-dried tomatoes, cut into slivers

1. Heat oil in skillet. Brown several pieces of chicken at a time in oil, but make sure not to crowd the skillet so the chicken can brown evenly.
2. Transfer chicken to slow cooker as it finishes browning.
3. Add garlic, wine, chicken broth, and basil to skillet. Bring to a boil. Scrape up any bits from the bottom of the pan.
4. Pour over chicken. Scatter tomatoes over chicken.
5. Cover and cook on low 4 to 6 hours.

15-minute prep

Red Pepper Chicken

makes 4 servings
ideal slow cooker: 4-quart

4 boneless, skinless chicken breast halves
15-oz. can black beans, drained
12-oz. jar roasted red bell peppers, undrained
14½-oz. can Mexican-style stewed tomatoes, undrained
1 large onion, chopped
½ tsp. salt
Black pepper to taste

1. Place chicken in slow cooker.
2. Combine beans, red peppers, stewed tomatoes, onion, salt, and pepper. Pour over chicken.
3. Cover and cook on high 2 to 3 hours or until chicken is no longer pink.
4. Serve over rice.

Southwestern Chicken

makes 6 servings
ideal slow cooker: 6-quart

2 15¼-oz. cans corn, drained
15-oz. can black beans, rinsed and drained
16-oz. jar chunky salsa, divided
6 boneless, skinless chicken breast halves
1 cup low-fat shredded Cheddar cheese

1. Combine corn, black beans, and ½ cup salsa in slow cooker.
2. Top with chicken. Pour remaining salsa over chicken.
3. Cover and cook on high 3 to 4 hours or on high 1 hour and then on low 5 to 6 hours.

4. Sprinkle with cheese. Cover 5 minutes for cheese to melt. Serve over rice, if desired.

Chicken Tortilla Casserole

makes 8 to 10 servings
ideal slow cooker: 5- or 6-quart

4 whole boneless, skinless chicken breasts, cooked and cut in 1-inch pieces (reserve ¼ cup broth chicken was cooked in)
10 6-inch flour tortillas, cut in strips about ½ x 2 inches
2 medium onions, chopped
1 tsp. canola oil
10¾-oz. can fat-free chicken broth
10¾-oz. can 98% fat-free cream of mushroom soup
2 4-oz. cans mild green chiles, chopped
1 egg
1 cup shredded low-fat Cheddar cheese

1. Pour reserved chicken broth in slow cooker sprayed with non-fat cooking spray.
2. Scatter half the tortilla strips in slow cooker.
3. Mix together remaining ingredients except the second half of tortilla strips and cheese.
4. Layer half the chicken mixture into the cooker, followed by the other half of the tortillas, followed by the rest of the chicken mix.
5. Cover and cook on high 3 to 5 hours or on low 4 to 6 hours.
6. Add the cheese to the top of the dish during the last 20 to 30 minutes of cooking.
7. Uncover and allow casserole to rest 15 minutes before serving.

Marinated Chinese
Chicken Salad

Aloha Chicken Cosmopolitan

makes 12 servings
ideal slow cooker: 5- or 6-quart

Dash of salt
5 lbs. boneless, skinless chicken
    breasts, cut in strips or cubed
1 cup frozen orange juice
1 cup coconut milk
1 cup soy sauce
¼ cup sesame oil

1. Lightly salt chicken and then refrigerate for 30 minutes.
2. Drain chicken of any juices that have gathered. Combine chicken with remaining 4 ingredients in slow cooker.

3. Cover and cook on high 1 hour and then on low 4 hours.
4. Serve with white rice.

Easy Chicken à la King

makes 4 servings
ideal slow cooker: 4-quart

1½ lbs. boneless, skinless chicken
    breasts
10¾-oz. can cream of chicken soup
3 Tbsp. all-purpose flour
¼ tsp. pepper
9-oz. pkg. frozen peas and onions,
    thawed and drained
2 Tbsp. chopped pimientos
½ tsp. paprika

1. Cut chicken into bite-size pieces and place in slow cooker.
2. Combine soup, flour, and pepper. Pour over chicken. Do not stir.
3. Cover and cook on high 2½ hours.
4. Stir in peas and onions, pimientos, and paprika.
5. Cover and cook on high 20 to 30 minutes.

variation:

• Add ¼ to ½ cup chopped green bell pepper to Step 2.

Marinated Chinese Chicken Salad

makes 8 servings
ideal slow cooker: 5-quart

3 garlic cloves, minced
1 Tbsp. grated fresh ginger
1 tsp. dried red pepper flakes
2 Tbsp. honey
3 Tbsp. low-sodium soy sauce
6 boneless, skinless chicken breast
    halves
½ cup rice wine vinegar
1 garlic clove, minced
1 tsp. grated fresh ginger
1 Tbsp. honey
1 large head iceberg lettuce,
    shredded
2 carrots, julienned
½ cup roasted peanuts, chopped
¼ cup chopped fresh cilantro
½ 6.75-oz. pkg. maifun noodles,
    fried in hot oil, or chow mein
    noodles

1. Stir together 3 minced garlic
cloves, 1 Tbsp. ginger, red pepper
flakes, 2 Tbsp. honey, and soy
sauce in a small bowl.
2. Place chicken in slow cooker
and pour soy sauce mixture over
chicken, coating each piece well.
3. Cover and cook on high 2 hours.
4. Remove chicken from slow
cooker and cool. Reserve juices.
Shred chicken into bite-size pieces.
5. In a small bowl, combine vinegar, 1 minced garlic clove, 1 tsp.
ginger, and 1 Tbsp. honey with
½ cup of juice from slow cooker to
make dressing.
6. In a large serving bowl, toss
together shredded chicken, lettuce,
carrots, peanuts, cilantro, and
noodles.
7. Just before serving, drizzle with
salad dressing. Toss well and serve.

Continental Chicken

makes 4 to 6 servings
ideal slow cooker: 5-quart

2¼-oz. pkg. dried beef
6 to 8 boneless, skinless chicken
    breast halves
6 to 8 bacon slices
10¾-oz. can cream of mushroom
    soup
¼ cup sour cream
¼ cup all-purpose flour

1. Arrange dried beef in slow
cooker.
2. Wrap each piece of chicken
with a strip of bacon. Place on top
of dried beef.
3. Combine soup, sour cream, and
flour. Pour over chicken.
4. Cover and cook on high 3 to 4
hours or on low 7 to 9 hours.
5. Serve over buttered noodles.

for the holidays
Comforting Chicken Stuffing

makes 4 to 6 servings
ideal slow cooker: 4-quart

2 6-oz. boxes stuffing mix
1 to 2 cups diced cooked chicken
10¾-oz. can cream of chicken soup
⅓ cup water or milk
½ tsp. salt
⅛ to ¼ tsp. pepper (optional)
4 Tbsp. (¼ cup) butter or
    margarine, melted (optional)

1. Prepare stuffing mix according
to package instructions. Spread in
bottom of greased slow cooker.
2. Combine chicken, soup, water,
and salt; add pepper, if desired.
Spread over stuffing. Top with
melted butter, if desired.

3. Cover and cook on high 2½ to
3 hours or on low 4 to 6 hours.
Loosen edges once or twice during
cooking or just before serving.
4. This is delicious served with
cole slaw and mixed fruit.

kid-friendly
Joyce's Chicken Tetrazzini

makes 4 servings
ideal slow cooker: 3- or 4-quart

2 cups diced cooked chicken
2 tsp. salt-free chicken bouillon
    powder
2 cups water
1 small onion, chopped
¼ cup Sauterne, white wine, or
    milk
½ cup slivered almonds
2 4-oz. cans sliced mushrooms,
    drained
10¾-oz. can 98% fat-free, reduced-
    sodium cream of mushroom
    soup
6 ozs. raw spaghetti, cooked
Parmesan cheese (optional)

1. Combine first 8 ingredients in
slow cooker.
2. Cover and cook on low 6 to 8
hours.
3. Serve over spaghetti. Sprinkle
with Parmesan cheese, if desired.

variations:

• Place spaghetti in large bak-
ing dish. Pour sauce in center.
Sprinkle with Parmesan cheese.
Broil until lightly browned.
• Add 10-oz. pkg. frozen peas to
Step 1.

Chicken Borscht

makes 8 servings
ideal slow cooker: 5- or 6-quart

1 qt. low-fat, low-sodium chicken
    broth
3 medium potatoes, cubed
3 carrots, sliced
2 celery ribs, sliced
Half a medium head of cabbage,
    chopped
2 cups frozen corn
2 cups green beans
1 medium onion, chopped
1 garlic clove, minced
2 cups low-sodium tomato juice
2 cups skinless chicken, cooked and
    diced or shredded
½ tsp. salt
¼ tsp. black pepper

1. Combine chicken broth,
potatoes, carrots, celery, cabbage,
corn, green beans, onion, garlic,
and tomato juice in slow cooker.
2. Cover and cook on low 8 to 10
hours.
3. Add chicken, salt, and pepper 30
minutes to 1 hour before serving.

White Chicken Chili

makes 6 to 8 servings
ideal slow cooker: 4- or 5-quart

2 whole skinless chicken breasts
6 cups water
2 onions, chopped
2 garlic cloves, minced
1 Tbsp. oil
2 to 4 4-oz. cans chopped green
    chiles
1 to 2 jalapeño peppers, diced
2 tsp. ground cumin
1½ tsp. dried oregano
¼ tsp. cayenne pepper
½ tsp. salt
3-lb. can navy beans, undrained
1 to 2 cups shredded cheese
Sour cream
Salsa

1. Place chicken in slow cooker.
Add water.
2. Cover and cook on high 1 hour
and then on low 1 to 2 hours or
until tender.
3. Remove chicken from slow
cooker. Cube and set aside.
4. Sauté onion and garlic in oil
in skillet. Add chiles, jalapeño
peppers, cumin, oregano, cayenne
pepper, and salt. Sauté 2 minutes.
Place in slow cooker.
5. Add navy beans.
6. Cover and cook on low 30 to 60
minutes.
7. Right before serving, add
chicken and cheese.
8. Serve topped with sour cream
and salsa. Corn bread or corn
chips are good go-alongs with
this chili.

variation:

• If you want to use dried beans,
use 3 cups navy beans and cover
with water in saucepan, soaking
overnight. In the morning, drain
and cover with fresh water. Cook
in saucepan on low 7 to 8 hours
or until tender. Drain excess
moisture and stir into chicken
and broth.

Spicy Chicken Rice Soup

makes 6 servings
ideal slow cooker: 3½- or 4-quart

4 cups low-fat, low-sodium chicken
    broth
2 cups cooked cubed chicken
2 celery ribs, chopped
2 medium carrots, chopped
1 medium-size green bell pepper,
    chopped
1 medium onion, chopped
¾ cup long grain rice, uncooked
¼ cup fresh parsley or cilantro,
    minced
½ tsp. salt
½ tsp. black pepper
½ tsp. dried oregano
¼ tsp. ground cumin
¼ tsp. crushed red pepper flakes
    (optional)

1. Combine all ingredients in slow
cooker.
2. Cover and cook on high until
boiling point, about 2 hours.
3. Reduce heat to low for 1½ hours
or just until rice and vegetables are
tender.

Chicken Gumbo

15-minute prep

makes 6 to 8 servings
ideal slow cooker: 3- or 4-quart

1 large onion, chopped
3 to 4 garlic cloves, minced
1 green bell pepper, diced
2 cups okra, sliced
2 cups tomatoes, chopped
4 cups chicken broth
1 lb. boneless, skinless chicken
    breast halves, cut in 1-inch
    pieces
2 tsp. Old Bay Seasoning
Cooked rice

1. Combine all ingredients except rice in slow cooker.
2. Cover and cook on high 3 to 4 hours or on high 1 hour and then on low 6 to 8 hours.
3. Serve over rice.

Joy's Brunswick Stew

15-minute prep

makes 8 servings
ideal slow cooker: 4-quart

1 lb. boneless, skinless chicken
    breast halves, cut in bite-size
    pieces
2 potatoes, thinly sliced
10¾-oz. can tomato soup
16-oz. can stewed tomatoes
10-oz. pkg. frozen corn
10-oz. pkg. frozen lima beans
3 Tbsp. onion flakes
¼ tsp. salt
⅛ tsp. pepper

1. Combine all ingredients in slow cooker.
2. Cover and cook on high 2 hours and then on low 2 hours.

Turkey Macaroni

makes 6 servings
ideal slow cooker: 5-quart

1 tsp. oil
1½ lbs. 99%-fat-free ground turkey
2 10¾-oz. cans low-sodium tomato
    soup, undiluted
16-oz. can whole-kernel corn,
    drained
½ cup chopped onion
4-oz. can sliced mushrooms,
    drained
2 Tbsp. ketchup
1 Tbsp. prepared mustard
¼ tsp. pepper
¼ tsp. garlic powder
2 cups dry macaroni, cooked and
    drained

1. Heat oil in medium skillet. Brown turkey. Drain.
2. Stir together all ingredients except macaroni in slow cooker.
3. Cover and cook on high 3 to 4 hours or on low 4 to 6 hours. Stir in cooked and drained macaroni 15 minutes before serving.

Lemony Turkey Breast

makes 12 servings
ideal slow cooker: 6-quart

5-lb. bone-in turkey breast, cut in
    half and skin removed
1 medium lemon, halved
1 tsp. lemon pepper seasoning
1 tsp. garlic salt
4 tsp. cornstarch
½ cup fat-free, low-sodium chicken
    broth

1. Place turkey, meaty side up, in slow cooker sprayed with cooking spray.
2. Squeeze half of lemon over turkey. Sprinkle with lemon pepper and garlic salt.
3. Place lemon halves under turkey.
4. Cover and cook on high 1 hour and then on low 3 to 5 hours.
5. Remove turkey. Discard lemons.
6. Allow turkey to rest 15 minutes before slicing.
7. To make gravy, pour cooking liquid into a cup. Skim the fat. In saucepan, combine cornstarch and broth until smooth. Gradually stir in cooking liquid. Bring to a boil. Cook and stir for 2 minutes. Serve over turkey slices.

Zucchini and Turkey Dish

makes 6 servings
ideal slow cooker: 3- or 4-quart

3 cups sliced zucchini
1 small onion, chopped
¼ tsp. salt
1 cup cubed cooked turkey
2 fresh tomatoes, sliced, or 14½-oz.
    can diced tomatoes
½ tsp. dried oregano
1 tsp. dried basil
¼ cup freshly grated Parmesan
    cheese
6 Tbsp. shredded provolone cheese
¾ cup Pepperidge Farm stuffing

1. Combine zucchini, onion, salt, turkey, tomatoes, oregano, and basil in slow cooker. Mix well.
2. Top with cheeses and stuffing.
3. Cover and cook on low 8 to 9 hours.

Turkey Burritos

Turkey Burritos

makes 8 servings
ideal slow cooker: 3-quart
pictured on cover

30-oz. roast turkey breast
    tenderloins (we used Jennie-O)
8-oz. can no-salt-added tomato
    sauce
4.5-oz. can chopped green chiles
1 cup chopped onions
2 Tbsp. Worcestershire sauce
1 Tbsp. chili powder
¼ tsp. garlic powder
8 8-inch flour tortillas
1 head iceberg lettuce, shredded
    (optional)
Green onions, chopped (optional)
Ripe olives, sliced (optional)
3 roma tomatoes, seeded and
    chopped (optional)
Shredded Cheddar cheese
    (optional)

1. Place turkey in slow cooker.
2. Combine tomato sauce, chiles, onions, Worcestershire sauce, chili powder, and garlic powder. Pour over turkey.
3. Cover and cook on low 6 to 8 hours.
4. Remove turkey from cooker. Shred with a fork and return to cooker; mix well.
5. Using a slotted spoon, spoon about ½ cup turkey mixture down center of each tortilla. Fold the bottom of each tortilla over filling and roll up. Add lettuce, green onions, olives, tomatoes, and Cheddar cheese, if desired.

Turkey Chili

makes 6 to 8 servings
ideal slow cooker: 4-quart

2 lbs. ground turkey, browned and
    drained
16-oz. can pinto or kidney beans
2 cups chopped fresh tomatoes
2 cups no-salt-added tomato sauce
1 garlic clove, minced
16-oz. can Rotel tomatoes
1-oz. pkg. Williams chili seasoning

1. Crumble ground turkey in slow cooker.
2. Add remaining ingredients. Mix well.
3. Cover and cook on low 6 to 8 hours.

Stuffed Turkey Breast

makes 12 servings
ideal slow cooker: 5- or 6-quart

¼ cup margarine, melted
1 small onion, finely chopped
½ cup finely chopped celery
2½-oz. pkg. croutons with real
    bacon bits
1 cup chicken broth
2 Tbsp. fresh minced parsley
½ tsp. poultry seasoning
1 whole uncooked turkey breast or
    2 halves (about 5 lbs.), skin and
    visible fat removed
Salt to taste
Pepper to taste
24- x 26-inch piece of cheesecloth
    for each breast half
Dry white wine

1. Combine margarine, onion, celery, croutons, broth, parsley, and poultry seasoning.
2. Cut turkey breast in thick slices from breastbone to rib cage, leaving slices attached to bone (crosswise across breast).
3. Sprinkle turkey with salt and pepper.
4. Soak cheesecloth in wine. Place turkey on cheesecloth. Stuff crouton mixture into slits between turkey slices. Fold 1 end of cheesecloth over the other to cover meat. Place on metal rack or trivet in slow cooker.
5. Cover and cook on high 1 hour and then on low 5 to 7 hours or until tender. Pour additional wine over turkey during cooking.
6. Remove from pot and remove cheesecloth immediately. If you prefer the breast to be browner, remove from pot and brown in a

400° oven for 15 to 20 minutes. Let stand 10 minutes before slicing through and serving.

variation:

• Thicken the drippings, if you wish, for gravy. Mix together 3 Tbsp. cornstarch and ¼ cup cold water. When smooth, stir into broth (with turkey removed from cooker). Turn cooker to high and stir until cornstarch paste is dissolved. Allow to cook for about 10 minutes, until broth is thickened and smooth.

Italian Turkey Sandwiches

makes 10 servings
ideal slow cooker: 6-quart

5½-lb. bone-in turkey breast, cut in
    half and skin removed
½ cup chopped green bell pepper
1 medium onion, chopped
¼ cup chili sauce
3 Tbsp. white vinegar
2 Tbsp. dried oregano or Italian
    seasoning
4 tsp. beef bouillon granules

1. Place turkey breast, green pepper, and onion in slow cooker.
2. Combine chili sauce, vinegar, oregano, and bouillon. Pour over turkey and vegetables.
3. Cover and cook on high 1 hour and then on low 3 to 4 hours or until meat juices run clear and vegetables are tender.
4. Remove turkey, reserving cooking liquid. Shred turkey with 2 forks.
5. Return turkey to cooking juices.

6. Using a slotted spoon, spoon approximately ½ cup turkey onto a Kaiser or hard sandwich roll.

Turkey Meatballs and Gravy

makes 8 servings
ideal slow cooker: 3-quart

2 eggs, beaten
¾ cup bread crumbs
½ cup finely chopped onion
½ cup finely chopped celery
2 Tbsp. chopped fresh parsley
¼ tsp. pepper
⅛ tsp. garlic powder
1 tsp. salt
2 lbs. ground raw turkey
1½ Tbsp. cooking oil
10¾-oz. can cream of mushroom
    soup
1 cup water
⅞-oz. pkg. turkey gravy mix
½ tsp. dried thyme
2 bay leaves

1. Combine eggs, bread crumbs, onion, celery, parsley, pepper, garlic powder, salt, and turkey. Shape into 1½-inch balls.
2. Brown meatballs in oil in skillet. Drain meatballs and place in slow cooker.
3. Combine soup, water, dry gravy mix, thyme, and bay leaves. Pour over meatballs.
4. Cover and cook on high 3 to 4 hours or on low 6 to 8 hours. Discard bay leaves before serving.
5. Serve over mashed potatoes or buttered noodles.

Red Beans and Pasta

meatless main dishes

Red Beans and Pasta

makes 6 to 8 servings
ideal slow cooker: 4- or 5-quart

3 14-oz. cans vegetable broth
½ tsp. ground cumin
1 Tbsp. chili powder
1 garlic clove, minced
Half a large green bell pepper, diced
Half a large red bell pepper, diced
1 medium onion, diced
15-oz. can red beans, rinsed and drained
8 ozs. uncooked spiral pasta
Chopped fresh parsley or cilantro

1. Combine broth, cumin, chili powder, garlic, diced vegetables, and beans in slow cooker.
2. Cover and cook on low 4 to 5 hours.
3. Stir together well. Add pasta and cook 15 minutes or until pasta is tender. Sprinkle with chopped parsley or cilantro before serving.

Tuscan Garlicky Bean Soup

makes 8 to 10 servings
ideal slow cooker: 4-quart

1 lb. dry great Northern or other dry white beans
1 qt. water
1 qt. 99%-fat-free, lower-sodium vegetable broth
2 garlic cloves, minced
¼ cup chopped parsley
3 Tbsp. olive oil
1¼ tsp. salt
½ tsp. pepper

1. Place beans in large soup pot. Cover with water and bring to a boil. Cook 2 minutes. Remove from heat. Cover pot and allow to stand for 1 hour. Drain, discarding water.
2. Combine beans, 1 qt. fresh water, and broth in slow cooker.
3. Sauté garlic and parsley in olive oil in skillet. Stir into slow cooker. Add salt and pepper.
4. Cover and cook on low 8 to 10 hours or until beans are tender.

Onion Soup

makes 6 to 8 servings
ideal slow cooker: 3- or 4-quart

3 medium onions, thinly sliced
¼ cup butter
1 tsp. salt
1 Tbsp. sugar
2 Tbsp. all-purpose flour
1 qt. vegetable broth
½ cup dry white wine
Slices of French bread
Grated Swiss or Parmesan cheese

1. Sauté onion in butter in covered skillet until soft. Uncover. Add salt and sugar. Cook 15 minutes. Stir in flour. Cook 3 minutes more.
2. Combine onion mixture, broth, and wine in slow cooker.
3. Cover and cook on low 6 to 8 hours.
4. Toast bread. Sprinkle with grated cheese and then broil.
5. Dish soup into individual bowls; then float a slice of broiled bread on top of each serving.

Aunt Thelma's
Homemade Soup

Minestra di Ceci

makes 4 to 6 servings
ideal slow cooker: 5-quart

1 lb. dry chickpeas
1 fresh rosemary sprig
10 fresh sage leaves
2 Tbsp. salt
1 or 2 large garlic cloves, minced
Olive oil
1 cup small dry pasta, your choice
    of shape, or dry penne

1. Wash chickpeas. Place in slow cooker. Fill cooker with water, and soak peas, along with rosemary, sage, and salt, 8 hours.
2. Drain water. Remove and discard herbs.
3. Refill slow cooker with water to 1 inch above peas.
4. Cover and cook on low 5 hours.
5. Sauté garlic in olive oil in skillet until translucent.
6. Puree half of peas, along with several cups of broth from cooker,

in blender. Return puree to slow cooker. Add garlic.
7. Boil pasta in saucepan until al dente, about 5 minutes. Drain. Add to beans.
8. Cover and cook on high 30 minutes to 1 hour or until pasta is tender and heated through but not mushy.

variation:

• Add ½ tsp. black pepper to Step 1, if you like.

Aunt Thelma's Homemade Soup

editor's favorite • entertaining

makes 10 to 12 servings
ideal slow cooker: 6-quart

7 cups water
4 vegetable bouillon cubes
1 cup thinly sliced carrots
1-lb. pkg. frozen peas
1-lb. pkg. frozen corn
1-lb. pkg. frozen lima beans
1 bay leaf
¼ tsp. dill seeds
28-oz. can diced tomatoes
1 cup diced potatoes
1 cup chopped onions
2 to 3 tsp. salt
½ tsp. dried basil
¼ tsp. pepper
2 Tbsp. cornstarch
¼ cup cold water

1. Combine all ingredients except cornstarch and ¼ cup water in slow cooker.
2. Cover and cook on high 3½ hours or until vegetables are tender.
3. Stir together cornstarch and cold water until smooth. Remove 1 cup broth from cooker and mix with cornstarch mixture. When smooth, stir into soup. Cover and continue cooking another 30 minutes. Remove bay leaf before serving.
4. Serve with a loaf of fresh Italian bread.

Lentil-Tomato Stew

editor's favorite

makes 8 servings
ideal slow cooker: 6-quart

3 cups water
28-oz. can low-sodium peeled Italian tomatoes, undrained
6-oz. can low-sodium tomato paste
½ cup dry red wine
¾ tsp. dried basil
¾ tsp. dried thyme
½ tsp. dried crushed red pepper
1 lb. dried lentils, rinsed and drained with stones removed
1 large onion, chopped
4 medium carrots, cut in ½-inch rounds
4 medium celery ribs, cut in ½-inch slices
3 garlic cloves, minced
1 tsp. salt
Fresh basil or parsley, chopped

1. Combine water, tomatoes with juice, tomato paste, wine, basil, thyme, and crushed red pepper in slow cooker.
2. Break up tomatoes with a wooden spoon; stir to blend them and the paste into the mixture.
3. Add lentils, onion, carrots, celery, and garlic.
4. Cover and cook on high 4 to 5 hours or on low 10 to 12 hours.
5. Stir in salt.
6. Serve in bowls and sprinkle with chopped basil or parsley.

Winter Squash and White Bean Stew

healthy for you

makes 6 servings
ideal slow cooker: 4-quart

1 cup chopped onions
1 Tbsp. olive oil
½ tsp. ground cumin
¼ tsp. ground cinnamon
1 garlic clove, minced
3 cups cubed butternut squash
1½ cups vegetable broth
19-oz. can cannellini beans, drained
14½-oz. can diced tomatoes, undrained
1 Tbsp. chopped fresh cilantro

1. Combine all ingredients in slow cooker.
2. Cover and cook on high 1 hour and then on low 2 to 3 hours.

variations:

• Beans can be pureed in blender and added during the last hour of cooking.
• Eight ozs. dried beans can be soaked overnight, cooked until soft, and used in place of canned beans.

Garden Chili

Garden Chili

makes 10 servings
ideal slow cooker: 3½- or 4-quart

¾ lb. onions, chopped
1 tsp. minced garlic
1 Tbsp. olive oil
¾ cup chopped celery
1 large carrot, peeled and thinly
   sliced
1 large green bell pepper, chopped
1 small zucchini, sliced
¼ lb. fresh mushrooms, sliced
1¼ cups water
14-oz. can kidney beans, drained
14-oz. can low-sodium diced
   tomatoes with juice
1 tsp. lemon juice
⅛ tsp. dried oregano
1 tsp. ground cumin
1 tsp. chili powder
1 tsp. salt
1 tsp. black pepper

1. Sauté onion and garlic in oil in
a large skillet over medium heat
until tender.
2. Add remaining veggies. Sauté 2
to 3 minutes. Place in slow cooker.
3. Add remaining ingredients.
4. Cover and cook on low 6 to 8
hours.

kid-friendly

Cheese and Potato Bake

makes 8 servings
ideal slow cooker: 4-quart

2-lb. bag frozen hash browns,
   thawed
10¾-oz. can Cheddar cheese soup
10¾-oz. can cream of onion soup
1 cup milk
2.8-oz. can French-fried onion rings
½ cup grated Cheddar cheese

healthy for you

Mjeddrah or Esau's Lentil Soup

makes 12 servings
ideal slow cooker: 4-quart

1 cup chopped carrots
1 cup diced celery
2 cups chopped onion
1 Tbsp. olive oil or butter
2 cups uncooked brown rice
1 Tbsp. olive oil or butter
6 cups water
1 lb. lentils, washed and drained
Garden salad
Vinaigrette

1. Sauté carrots, celery, and onion in
1 Tbsp. oil in skillet. When soft and
translucent, place in slow cooker.
2. Brown rice in 1 Tbsp. oil until
dry. Add to slow cooker.
3. Stir in water and lentils.
4. Cover and cook on high 6 to 8
hours.
5. When thoroughly cooked,
serve in individual soup bowls.
Cover each with a serving of fresh
garden salad (lettuce, spinach
leaves, chopped tomatoes, minced
onions, chopped bell peppers,
sliced olives, sliced radishes). Pour
favorite vinaigrette over all.

1. Combine hash browns, soups, and milk in slow cooker. Mix well.
2. Top with half can of onion rings.
3. Cover and cook on low 5 to 7 hours. Sprinkle with cheese and remaining onion rings and cook 1 more hour before serving.

15-minute prep

Norma's Vegetarian Chili

makes 8 to 10 servings
ideal slow cooker: 4- or 5-quart

2 Tbsp. oil
2 cups minced celery
1½ cups chopped green bell
  pepper
1 cup minced onion
4 garlic cloves, minced
5½ cups stewed tomatoes
2 1-lb. cans kidney beans, undrained
1½ to 2 cups raisins
¼ cup wine vinegar
1 Tbsp. chopped parsley
2 tsp. salt
1½ tsp. dried oregano
1½ tsp. cumin
¼ tsp. black pepper
¼ tsp. Tabasco sauce
1 bay leaf
¾ cup cashews
1 cup grated cheese (optional)

1. Combine all ingredients except cashews and cheese in slow cooker.
2. Cover and cook on low 8 hours. Add cashews and simmer 30 minutes. Remove bay leaf.
3. Garnish individual servings with grated cheese, if desired.

Apple Bean Bake

makes 12 servings
ideal slow cooker: 4- or 5-quart

4 Tbsp. margarine
2 large unpeeled Granny Smith
  apples, cubed
¼ cup brown sugar
2 Tbsp. granulated sugar
Brown sugar substitute to equal
  2 Tbsp.
White sugar substitute to equal
  1 Tbsp.
½ cup no-salt-added ketchup
1 tsp. ground cinnamon
1 Tbsp. molasses
24-oz. can great Northern beans,
  undrained
24-oz. can pinto beans, undrained

1. Melt margarine in skillet. Add apples and cook until tender.
2. Stir in brown sugar, sugar, and sugar substitutes. Cook until they melt. Stir in ketchup, cinnamon, and molasses.
3. Add beans. Mix well. Pour into slow cooker.
4. Cover and cook on high 2 to 4 hours.

Tofu and Vegetables

makes 6 servings
ideal slow cooker: 4- or 5-quart

16 ozs. firm tofu, drained and
  crumbled
½ cup chopped onion
½ cup chopped celery
2 cups chopped bok choy
2 cups chopped napa cabbage
½ cup pea pods, cut in half

1. Combine all ingredients in slow cooker.
2. Cook on low 6 hours.

entertaining

Arroz con Queso

makes 6 to 8 servings
ideal slow cooker: 4-quart

14½-oz. can whole tomatoes,
  mashed
15-oz. can Mexican-style beans,
  undrained
1½ cups uncooked long grain rice
3 ozs. grated reduced-fat Monterey
  Jack cheese
1 large onion, finely chopped
1 cup low-fat cottage cheese
4¼-oz. can chopped green chiles,
  drained
1 Tbsp. canola oil
3 garlic cloves, minced
3 ozs. grated reduced-fat Monterey
  Jack cheese

1. Combine all ingredients except final 3 ozs. of cheese. Pour into well greased slow cooker.
2. Cover and cook on low 6 to 9 hours.
3. Sprinkle with remaining cheese before serving.
4. Serve with salsa.

Brown Jug Soup

soups and stews

Brown Jug Soup

makes 10 to 12 servings
ideal slow cooker: 5-quart

10½-oz. can chicken broth

2 pkgs. sodium-free chicken
   bouillon

1 qt. water

3 to 4 celery ribs, diced

2 medium onions, diced

4 cups diced potatoes

3 cups diced carrots

10-oz. pkg. frozen whole-kernel
   corn, thawed

2 10¾-oz. cans 98%-fat-free,
   reduced-sodium cream of
   chicken soup

4 ozs. shredded sharp Cheddar
   cheese

1. Combine all ingredients except
cheese in slow cooker.
2. Cover and cook on low 8 to
10 hours or until vegetables are
tender.
3. Just before serving, add cheese.
Stir until cheese is melted.

Quick-to-Mix Vegetable Soup

makes 4 servings
ideal slow cooker: 2-quart

2 cups mixed frozen sliced
   vegetables, thawed

¾ cup fat-free, low-sodium beef
   gravy

16-oz. can diced tomatoes,
   undrained

¼ cup dry red wine

½ cup diced onions

1 tsp. crushed garlic

¼ tsp. pepper

½ cup water

1. Combine all ingredients in slow
cooker.
2. Cover and cook on high 5 hours
or on low 7 hours.

note:

• If your diet permits, you may
want to add ¼ to ½ tsp. salt to
Step 1.

Frances's Hearty Vegetable Soup

makes 10 servings
ideal slow cooker: 6-quart

1 lb. round steak, cut in ½-inch
   pieces

14½-oz. can diced tomatoes

3 cups water

2 potatoes, peeled and cubed

2 onions, sliced

3 celery ribs, sliced

2 carrots, sliced

3 beef bouillon cubes

½ tsp. dried basil

½ tsp. dried oregano

¼ tsp. pepper

1½ cups frozen mixed vegetables
   or your choice of frozen
   vegetables

1. Combine first 3 ingredients in
slow cooker.
2. Cover and cook on high 6 hours.
3. Add remaining ingredients.
Cover and cook on high 2 hours
more or until meat and vegetables
are tender.

Hearty Alphabet Soup

Hearty Alphabet Soup

makes 6 servings
ideal slow cooker: 3-quart

½ lb. beef stew meat or round
    steak, trimmed of fat and
    cubed
14½-oz. can stewed tomatoes
    (2 cups)
8-oz. can tomato sauce
1 cup water
1-oz. envelope dry onion soup mix
10-oz. pkg. frozen vegetables,
    thawed
½ cup uncooked alphabet noodles
2 cups water (optional)

1. Combine meat, tomatoes,
tomato sauce, water, and soup mix
in slow cooker.
2. Cover and cook on high 1 hour
and then on low 4 to 6 hours.
Turn to high.
3. Stir in vegetables and noodles.
Add 2 cups water if mixture is too
thick.
4. Cover and cook on high 30
minutes or until vegetables are
tender.

Beef Dumpling Soup

makes 5 to 6 servings
ideal slow cooker: 5-quart

1 lb. beef stewing meat, cubed
1-oz. envelope dry onion soup mix
6 cups hot water
2 carrots, peeled and shredded
1 celery rib, finely chopped
1 tomato, peeled and chopped
1 cup buttermilk biscuit mix
1 Tbsp. finely chopped fresh
    parsley
6 Tbsp. milk

1. Place meat in slow cooker. Sprinkle with onion soup mix. Pour hot water over meat.
2. Add carrots, celery, and tomato.
3. Cover and cook on high 1 hour then on low 2 to 4 hours or until meat is tender.
4. Combine biscuit mix and parsley. Stir in milk with fork until moistened. Drop dumplings by teaspoonfuls into pot.
5. Cover and cook on high 30 minutes.

variation:

: • Increase the flavor of the broth by adding 2 minced garlic cloves, ½ tsp. dried basil, and ¼ tsp. dried dill weed to Step 2.

Hamburger Lentil Soup

makes 8 servings
ideal slow cooker: 5- or 6-quart

1 lb. ground beef
½ cup chopped onions
4 carrots, diced
3 celery ribs, diced
1 garlic clove, minced, or 1 tsp. garlic powder
4 cups tomato juice
1 Tbsp. salt
2 cups dry lentils, washed and stones removed
4 cups water
½ tsp. dried marjoram
1 Tbsp. brown sugar

1. Brown ground beef and onion in skillet. Drain.
2. Combine all ingredients in slow cooker.
3. Cover and cook on high 4 to 6 hours or on low 8 to 10 hours.

Taco Soup with Pinto Beans

makes 10 to 12 servings
ideal slow cooker: 6-quart

1 lb. ground beef
1 large onion, finely chopped
3 14-oz. cans pinto beans
14-oz. can tomatoes with chiles, undrained
14½-oz. can chopped tomatoes, undrained
15-oz. can tomato sauce
1-oz. pkg. dry Hidden Valley Ranch Dressing mix
1.25-oz. pkg. dry taco seasoning mix
15¼-oz. can whole-kernel corn, drained

1. Brown beef and onion in skillet. Drain.
2. Combine all ingredients in slow cooker.
3. Cover and cook on low 4 hours or until ingredients are heated through.

healthy for you

Dottie's Creamy Steak Soup

makes 8 servings
ideal slow cooker: 4-quart

½ lb. 85%-lean ground beef
Half a large onion, chopped
12-oz. can low-sodium V-8 vegetable juice
3 medium potatoes, diced
10¾-oz. can 98%-fat-free, reduced-sodium cream of mushroom soup
10¾-oz. can cream of celery soup
16-oz. pkg. frozen mixed vegetables, or your choice of frozen vegetables, thawed
½ to ¾ tsp. pepper

1. Sauté beef and onion in skillet. Drain.
2. Combine all ingredients in slow cooker.
3. Cover and cook on low 8 to 10 hours.

Beef-Barley-Lentil Soup

makes 10 servings
ideal slow cooker: 5- or 6-quart

1 lb. extra-lean ground beef
1 medium onion, chopped
2 cups cubed potatoes
1 cup chopped celery
1 cup diced carrot
1 cup dried lentils, rinsed
½ cup medium pearl barley
8 cups water
2 tsp. beef bouillon granules
½ tsp. salt
½ tsp. lemon pepper seasoning
2 14½-oz. cans low-sodium stewed tomatoes, undrained

1. Brown ground beef with onion in a skillet. Drain.
2. Combine all ingredients except tomatoes in slow cooker.
3. Cover and cook on low 6 hours or until tender.
4. Add tomatoes. Cook on low 2 hours more.

note:

: • For added zest, you may want to increase the lemon pepper seasoning to 1 tsp. You may also want to add ½ tsp. dried basil and ½ tsp. dried thyme to Step 2.

Barbara Jean's Burger Soup

makes 8 servings
ideal slow cooker: 4- or 5-quart

2 lbs. extra-lean ground beef
5 cups water
1 medium onion, chopped
14½-oz. can diced tomatoes
½ cup chopped celery
3 Yukon gold potatoes, cubed
½ cup chopped carrot
½ cup frozen corn, thawed
¼ tsp. salt
¼ tsp. freshly ground pepper
½ tsp. dried basil
½ cup frozen peas, thawed

1. Brown beef in non-stick skillet.
2. Combine all ingredients except peas in slow cooker.
3. Cover and cook on low 6 to 8 hours.
4. Stir in peas 30 minutes before serving.

Ruth's Split Pea Soup

makes 8 servings
ideal slow cooker: 4-quart

1 bag (2¼ cups) dried split peas
½ lb. bulk sausage, browned and drained
6 cups water
2 medium potatoes, diced
1 onion, chopped
½ tsp. dried marjoram or thyme
½ tsp. pepper

1. Wash and sort dried peas, removing any stones.
2. Combine all ingredients in slow cooker.
3. Cover and cook on low 12 hours.

Chicken Corn Soup

makes 4 to 6 servings
ideal slow cooker: 4-quart

2 boneless, skinless chicken breast halves, cubed
1 onion, chopped
1 garlic clove, minced
2 carrots, sliced
2 celery ribs, chopped
2 medium potatoes, cubed
1 tsp. mixed dried herbs
⅓ cup tomato sauce
12-oz. can cream-style corn
14-oz. can whole-kernel corn, undrained
1 Tbsp. sodium-free chicken bouillon powder
3 cups water
¼ cup chopped fresh Italian parsley
¼ tsp. pepper

1. Combine all ingredients except parsley and pepper in slow cooker.
2. Cover and cook on high 1 hour and then on low 6 to 8 hours or until chicken is tender.
3. Add parsley and pepper 30 minutes before serving.

Double Cheese Cauliflower Soup

makes 6 servings
ideal slow cooker: 3½- or 4-quart

4 cups cauliflower pieces (1 small head)
2 cups water
8-oz. pkg. cream cheese, cubed
5 oz. American cheese spread
¼ lb. dried beef, torn into strips or shredded
½ cup potato flakes or buds

1. Combine cauliflower and water in saucepan. Bring to boil. Set aside.
2. Heat slow cooker on low. Add cream cheese and cheese spread. Pour in cauliflower and water. Stir cheese until dissolved and thoroughly mixed with cauliflower.
3. Add dried beef and potato flakes. Mix well.
4. Cover and cook on low 2 to 3 hours.

Vegetable-Beef Soup

makes 8 servings
ideal slow cooker: 4-quart

1 lb. extra-lean ground beef
14½-oz. can low-sodium stewed tomatoes
10¾-oz. can low-sodium tomato soup
1 onion, chopped
2 cups water
15½-oz. can garbanzo beans, drained
15¼-oz. can whole-kernel corn, drained
14½-oz. can sliced carrots, drained
1 cup diced potatoes
1 cup chopped celery
½ tsp. salt
¼ tsp. black pepper
Chopped garlic to taste (optional)

1. Sauté ground beef in non-stick skillet.
2. Combine all ingredients in slow cooker. Cover and cook on low 4 to 6 hours.

editor's favorite

Berenice's Favorite Chili

makes 6 servings
ideal slow cooker: 5- or 6-quart

2 16-oz. cans red kidney beans, drained
2 14½-oz. cans diced tomatoes
2 lbs. coarsely ground chuck, browned and drained
2 medium onions, coarsely chopped
1 green bell pepper, coarsely chopped
2 garlic cloves, minced
2½ Tbsp. chili powder
1 tsp. black pepper
2 tsp. salt
Toppings: sour cream, green onion slices, shredded Cheddar cheese

1. Combine first 9 ingredients in slow cooker. Stir once.
2. Cover and cook on high 4 to 5 hours or on low 8 to 10 hours.
3. Top individual servings with sour cream, green onions, and cheese. Serve with tortilla chips.

variation:

• Increase proportion of tomatoes in chili by adding 8-oz. can tomato sauce before cooking.

Berenice's
Favorite Chili

Corn Chili

makes 4 to 6 servings
ideal slow cooker: 4-quart

1 lb. ground beef
½ cup chopped onion
½ cup chopped green bell pepper
¼ tsp. salt
⅛ tsp. black pepper
¼ tsp. dried thyme
14½-oz. can diced tomatoes with Italian herbs
6-oz. can tomato paste
6-oz. can water
2 cups frozen whole-kernel corn
16-oz. can kidney beans
1 Tbsp. chili powder
Sour cream (optional)
Shredded cheese (optional)

1. Sauté ground beef, onion, and green pepper in deep saucepan. Drain and season with salt, black pepper, and thyme.
2. Stir in tomatoes, tomato paste, water, and corn. Heat until corn is thawed. Add kidney beans and chili powder. Pour into slow cooker.
3. Cover and cook on low 5 to 6 hours.
4. Top individual servings with dollops of sour cream or sprinkle with shredded cheese, if desired.

soups and stews **131**

**Caribbean-Style
Black Bean Soup**

Caribbean-Style Black Bean Soup

**makes 8 servings
ideal slow cooker: 4-quart**

1 lb. dried black beans, rinsed and
    stones removed
3 onions, chopped
1 green bell pepper, chopped
4 garlic cloves, minced
1 lean ham hock or ¾ cup lean
    cubed ham
1 Tbsp. oil
1 Tbsp. ground cumin
1 to 2 tsp. dried oregano, according
    to your taste preference
¼ to 1 tsp. dried thyme, according
    to your taste preference
1 tsp. salt
½ tsp. black pepper
3 cups water
2 Tbsp. vinegar
½ cup fat-free sour cream
Fresh cilantro

1. Soak beans overnight in 4 qts. water. Drain.
2. Combine soaked beans, onion, green pepper, garlic, ham hock, oil, cumin, oregano, thyme, salt, black pepper, and 3 cups water. Stir well.
3. Cover and cook on high 4 to 5 hours or on low 8 to 10 hours.
4. For a thick soup, remove half of cooked bean mixture; puree until smooth in blender or mash with potato masher. Return to cooker. If you like a thinner soup, leave as is.
5. Add vinegar and stir well. If you used a ham hock, debone the ham, cut in bite-size pieces, and return to soup.
6. Serve soup in bowls with a dollop of sour cream in the middle of each individual serving and top with fresh cilantro.

15-minute prep

Kielbasa Soup

**makes 8 servings
ideal slow cooker: 4-quart**

16-oz. pkg. frozen mixed
    vegetables or your choice of
    vegetables
6-oz. can tomato paste
1 medium onion, chopped
3 medium potatoes, diced
12 ozs. low-fat kielbasa, cut in
    ¼-inch pieces
4 qts. water
Fresh parsley

1. Combine all ingredients except parsley in slow cooker.
2. Cover and cook on low 12 hours.
3. Garnish individual servings with fresh parsley.

San Antonio-Style Tortilla Soup

**makes 9 to 10 servings
ideal slow cooker: 5-quart**

1 Tbsp. olive oil
1 onion, chopped
2 garlic cloves, minced
2 tsp. ground cumin
2 14-oz. cans fat-free chicken broth
2 15-oz. cans stewed tomatoes
1 Tbsp. minced jalapeño pepper
    (remove seeds to reduce heat)
¼ tsp. black pepper
2 cups (about 1½ lbs.) boneless,
    skinless chicken breast halves,
    uncooked and cubed
2 cups water

1. Combine all ingredients in slow cooker.
2. Cover and cook on high 4 to 6 hours or on high 1 hour and then on low 4 to 6 hours.

Green Bean Soup

makes 6 servings
ideal slow cooker: 5-quart

1 meaty ham bone or 2 cups cubed
  ham
1½ qts. water
1 large onion, chopped
2 to 3 cups cut green beans
3 large carrots, sliced
2 large potatoes, peeled and cubed
1 Tbsp. minced fresh parsley
1 Tbsp. minced fresh summer savory
½ tsp. salt
¼ tsp. pepper
1 cup cream or milk

1. Combine all ingredients except
cream in slow cooker.
2. Cover and cook on high 4 to 6
hours.
3. Remove ham bone. Cut off meat
and return to slow cooker.
4. Turn to low. Stir in cream. Heat
through and serve.

Oriental Pork Soup

makes 6 servings
ideal slow cooker: 3- or 4-quart

1 lb. lean uncooked pork or
  chicken, cut in ½-inch cubes
2 medium carrots, cut in julienne
  strips
4 medium-size green onions,
  chopped
1 garlic clove, finely chopped
3 to 4 Tbsp. low-sodium soy
  sauce, according to your taste
  preference
½ tsp. finely chopped gingerroot
⅛ tsp. black pepper
10¾-oz. can fat-free, reduced-
  sodium beef broth
1 cup fresh mushrooms, sliced
1 cup bean sprouts

1. Cook meat in large non-stick
skillet over medium heat for 8 to
10 minutes. Stir occasionally.
2. Mix meat and remaining
ingredients except mushrooms
and bean sprouts in slow cooker.
3. Cover and cook on high 3 to 4
hours or on low 7 to 9 hours.
4. Stir in mushrooms and bean
sprouts.
5. Cover and cook on low 1 hour.

editor's favorite

Lentil Soup with Ham Bone

makes 6 to 8 servings
ideal slow cooker: 5-quart

1 lb. dried lentils, rinsed and
  drained
1 celery rib, chopped
1 large carrot, grated
½ cup chopped onion
1 bay leaf
¼ tsp. dried thyme
7 to 8 cups water
1 ham bone, thinly sliced kielbasa,
  or hot smoked sausage
¼ to ½ tsp. crushed red hot pepper
  flakes
Salt to taste
Pepper to taste

1. Combine all ingredients except
salt and pepper in slow cooker.
2. Cover and cook on low 8 to 9
hours. Remove bay leaf and ham
bone. Dice meat from bone and
return to cooker.
3. Season to taste with salt and
pepper.
4. Serve alone or over rice with
grated cheese on top.

Sauerkraut Soup

makes 10 servings
ideal slow cooker: 5-quart

Low-fat kielbasa, cut into ½-inch
  pieces
5 medium potatoes, cubed
2 large onions, chopped
2 large carrots, cut in ¼-inch slices
4 tsp. sodium-free chicken bouillon
  powder
4 cups water
32-oz. can or bag sauerkraut,
  rinsed and drained
6-oz. can tomato paste

1. Combine all ingredients in slow
cooker. Stir to combine.
2. Cover and cook on high 2 hours
and then on low 6 to 8 hours.
3. Serve with rye bread.

Wash-Day Stew

makes 14 servings
ideal slow cooker: 4- or 5-quart

1½ to 2 lbs. lean lamb or beef,
  trimmed of fat and cubed
2 15-oz. cans garbanzo beans,
  drained
2 15-oz. cans white beans, drained
2 medium onions, peeled and
  quartered
1 qt. water
½ tsp. salt
1 tomato, peeled and quartered
1 tsp. turmeric
3 Tbsp. fresh lemon juice
8 to 10 pita rounds

1. Combine all ingredients except
pitas in slow cooker.
2. Cover and cook on high 6 to 7
hours.
3. Lift stew from cooker with a
strainer spoon; stuff in pita rounds.

Irish Stew

makes 8 servings
ideal slow cooker: 4- or 5-quart

2 lbs. lean boneless lamb, cubed
1½ tsp. salt
¼ tsp. pepper
2 medium carrots, sliced
1 large onion, diced
3 medium potatoes, diced
1 bay leaf
2 cups water
¼ cup dry small pearl tapioca
15-oz. can small tender green peas

1. Spray slow cooker with cooking spray.
2. Place cubed lamb in the bottom of slow cooker. Sprinkle with salt and pepper.
3. Layer carrots, onion, potatoes, and bay leaf over lamb.
4. Stir in water and tapioca.
5. Cover and cook on high 1½ hours and then on low 7 hours.
6. Add peas and cook 1 more hour.
7. Remove bay leaf before serving.

note:

• For increased flavor, you may want to divide ½ tsp. Mrs. Dash seasoning among the layers of vegetables in Step 3.

Pirate Stew

makes 4 to 6 servings
ideal slow cooker: 4-quart

Arggh! Little ones will love digging into this playfully named hearty stew.

1 lb. ground beef
¾ cup sliced onion
¼ cup uncooked long grain rice
3 cups diced raw potatoes
1 cup diced celery
2 cups canned kidney beans, drained
½ tsp. salt
⅛ tsp. pepper
¼ tsp. chili powder
¼ tsp. Worcestershire sauce
1 cup tomato sauce
½ cup water

1. Brown ground beef and onion in skillet. Drain.
2. Layer ingredients in slow cooker in order listed.
3. Cover and cook on low 6 hours or until potatoes and rice are cooked.

variation:

• Add a layer of 2 cups sliced carrot between potatoes and celery.

Fresh Corn Chowder

makes 7 servings
ideal slow cooker: 3½- or 4-quart

4 large ears corn, cut off cob, or 1-lb. bag frozen whole-kernel corn, thawed
1 large onion, chopped
1 celery rib, chopped
1 Tbsp. butter or margarine
1½ cups cubed potatoes
1 cup water
2 tsp. chicken bouillon granules
¼ tsp. dried thyme
¼ tsp. pepper
6 Tbsp. all-purpose flour
3 cups fat-free milk

1. Combine all ingredients except flour and milk.
2. Cover and cook on low 8 to 9 hours or until potatoes are tender.
3. Stir together flour and milk until smooth. Stir into corn chowder slowly until thickened.

note:

• If your diet permits, you may want to add ½ tsp. salt to Step 1.

Cassoulet Chowder

makes 8 servings
ideal slow cooker: 3½- or 4-quart

1¼ cups dry pinto beans
4 cups water
½ lb. lean sausage, cut into ¼-inch slices, cooked and drained
2 cups cubed cooked lean chicken
2 cups cubed cooked lean ham
1½ cups sliced carrots
8-oz. can low-sodium tomato sauce
¾ cup dry red wine
½ cup chopped onions
½ tsp. garlic powder
1 bay leaf

1. Combine beans and water in large saucepan. Bring to boil. Reduce heat and simmer 1½ hours. Refrigerate beans and liquid 4 to 8 hours.

2. Combine all ingredients in slow cooker.

3. Cover and cook on high 4 hours or on low 8 to 10 hours. If the chowder seems too thin, remove lid during last 30 minutes of cooking time to allow it to thicken.

4. Remove bay leaf before serving.

Green Chile-Corn Chowder

makes 8 servings
ideal slow cooker: 4-quart

16-oz. can cream-style corn
3 potatoes, peeled and diced
2 Tbsp. chopped fresh chives
4-oz. can diced green chiles, drained
2-oz. jar chopped pimientos, drained
½ cup chopped cooked ham
2 10½-oz. cans 100% fat-free, lower-sodium chicken broth
Salt to taste
Pepper to taste
Tabasco sauce to taste
1 cup milk

1. Combine all ingredients except milk in slow cooker.

2. Cover and cook on low 7 to 8 hours or until potatoes are tender.

3. Stir in milk. Heat until hot.

4. Serve with homemade bread.

kid-friendly

Chicken Chowder

makes 4 servings
ideal slow cooker: 3½-quart

½ cup shredded carrots
1 cup fat-free milk
½ cup low-sodium chicken broth
¼ tsp. pepper
1 cup chopped onion
1 potato, peeled and cut into ½-inch chunks
½ lb. boneless, skinless chicken breast halves, cut into 1-inch cubes
2 15-oz. cans cream-style corn
½ cup dried potato flakes
½ cup shredded low-fat Cheddar cheese

1. Combine all ingredients except potato flakes and cheese in slow cooker.

2. Cover and cook on high 1 hour and then on low 3 to 5 hours or until potatoes are tender and chicken is thoroughly cooked.

3. Add potato flakes and stir well to blend.

4. Cook, uncovered, on high 5 to 10 minutes or until chowder has thickened and dried potato flakes have dissolved.

5. Top each serving with cheese.

note:

• For more zest, and if your diet allows, you may want to add ½ tsp. salt to Step 1. You may also want to add ½ tsp. dried thyme to Step 1.

entertaining

Black Bean Chili con Carne

makes 18 servings
ideal slow cooker: 2
(4- or 5-quart) cookers

1 lb. dried black beans
3 lbs. ground beef
2 large onions, chopped
1 green bell pepper, chopped
3 garlic cloves, minced
2 tsp. salt
1 tsp. black pepper
6-oz. can tomato paste
3 cups (or more) tomato juice
1 tsp. celery salt
1 Tbsp. Worcestershire sauce
1 tsp. dry mustard
Cayenne pepper to taste
Ground cumin to taste
3 Tbsp. chili powder

1. Cover beans with water and soak 8 hours or overnight. Rinse and drain.

2. Brown meat in batches in large skillet. Drain.

3. Combine all ingredients in a large bowl. Divide between slow cookers.

4. Cover and cook on low 8 hours.

5. Serve over salad greens or wrapped in tortillas, topped with lettuce and grated cheese.

Herb Rice (page 147)

side dishes

Barbecued Green Beans

makes 6 servings
ideal slow cooker: 3- or 4-quart

4 slices bacon
¼ cup chopped onion
½ cup ketchup
2 Tbsp. brown sugar
Brown sugar substitute to equal
    2 Tbsp.
3 tsp. Worcestershire sauce
⅛ tsp. salt
4 cups green beans

1. Brown bacon in skillet until crisp and then break into pieces.
2. Sauté onion in non-fat cooking spray in skillet.
3. Combine ketchup, brown sugar, sugar substitute, Worcestershire sauce, and salt. Stir into bacon and onion.
4. Pour mixture over green beans and mix lightly.
5. Pour into slow cooker. Cook on high 3 to 4 hours or on low 6 to 8 hours.

Home-Baked Beans

makes 15 to 25 servings
ideal slow cooker: 6-quart

2 lbs. (4 cups) dried navy or pea
    beans
1 lb. salt pork or bacon, chopped
1 lb. (2½ cups), or less, brown sugar
1-lb., 3-oz. can tomatoes
2 medium onions, chopped
2 Tbsp. prepared mustard
½ tsp. salt
½ tsp. pepper

1. Sort and wash beans. Cover with water 2 inches above beans. Let soak overnight. Simmer in salted water until tender. Drain. Save liquid.
2. Place pork in bottom of slow cooker.
3. Stir together brown sugar, tomatoes, onions, mustard, salt, and pepper. Alternately layer tomato mixture and beans over pork.
4. Add enough reserved liquid to cover beans.
5. Cover and cook on low 8 to 10 hours, stirring occasionally.

Dutch Green Beans

makes 12 servings
ideal slow cooker: 4- or 5-quart

6 slices bacon
4 medium onions, sliced
2 Tbsp. canola oil
2 qts. fresh, frozen, or canned
    green beans
4 cups diced fresh tomatoes
½ tsp. salt
¼ tsp. pepper

1. Brown bacon until crisp in skillet. Drain. Crumble bacon into small pieces.
2. Sauté onion in oil.
3. Combine all ingredients in slow cooker.
4. Cover and cook on low 4½ hours.

Green Beans with Dill

Green Beans with Dill

makes 8 servings
ideal slow cooker: 3½- or 4-quart

2 qts. (1½ lbs.) fresh small green
    beans
2 tsp. beef bouillon granules
½ tsp. dill seed
¼ cup water

1. Spray slow cooker with cooking
spray.
2. Combine all ingredients in slow
cooker and mix well.
3. Cover and cook on high 1 to 3
hours, depending on your liking.

note:

   • If you like, add 2 Tbsp. minced
   onions and 1 tsp. garlic salt to
   Step 2.

entertaining

No-Meat Baked Beans

makes 8 to 10 servings
ideal slow cooker: 3½-quart

1 lb. dried navy beans
6 cups water
1 small onion, chopped
¾ cup ketchup
¾ cup brown sugar
¾ cup water
1 tsp. dry mustard
2 Tbsp. dark molasses
1 tsp. salt

1. Soak beans in water overnight
in a large soup kettle. Cook beans
in water until soft, about 1½ hours.
Drain, discarding bean water.
2. Stir together all ingredients in
slow cooker.
3. Cover and cook on low 10 to
12 hours.

Barbecued Lima Beans

makes 10 servings
ideal slow cooker: 6-quart

1½ lbs. dried lima beans
6 cups water
2¼ cups chopped onions
1¼ cups brown sugar
1½ cups ketchup
13 drops Tabasco sauce
1 cup dark corn syrup
1 Tbsp. salt
½ lb. bacon, diced

1. Sort and wash beans. Place
beans and 6 cups water in Dutch
oven. Let soak overnight. Do not
drain.

2. Add onion. Bring to a boil.
Simmer 30 to 60 minutes or until
beans are tender. Drain beans,
reserving liquid.
3. Combine all ingredients except
bean liquid in slow cooker. Mix
well. Pour in enough bean liquid
so that beans are barely covered.
4. Cover and cook on high 4 to
6 hours or on low 10 hours. Stir
occasionally.

Creole Black Beans

makes 6 to 8 servings
ideal slow cooker: 4-quart

¾ lb. lean smoked sausage, sliced
    in ¼-inch pieces and browned
3 15-oz. cans black beans, drained
1½ cups chopped onions
1½ cups chopped green bell
    pepper
1½ cups chopped celery
4 garlic cloves, minced
2 tsp. dried thyme
1½ tsp. dried oregano
1½ tsp. black pepper
1 chicken bouillon cube
3 bay leaves
8-oz. can tomato sauce
1 cup water

1. Combine all ingredients in slow
cooker.
2. Cover and cook on high 4 hours
or on low 8 hours.
3. Remove bay leaves before
serving.

note:

• For a different consistency, you
may substitute a 14½-oz. can of
low-sodium stewed tomatoes for
the tomato sauce.
• This is tasty served over
steamed rice.

New Orleans Red Beans

makes 6 servings
ideal slow cooker: 3½-quart

2 cups dried kidney beans
5 cups water
¼ lb. lean hot sausage, cut into
    small pieces
2 onions, chopped
2 garlic cloves, minced
1 tsp. salt

1. Sort and wash beans. Combine
beans and water in saucepan. Boil
2 minutes. Remove from heat.
Soak 1 hour. Do not drain.
2. Brown sausage slowly in non-
stick skillet. Add onions, garlic,
and salt and sauté until tender.
3. Combine all ingredients, including the bean water, in slow cooker.
4. Cover and cook on low 8 to 10
hours. During last 20 minutes of
cooking, stir frequently and mash
beans lightly with spoon to make
desired consistency.
5. Serve over hot cooked white
rice.

note:

• Offer salsa as a condiment with
this New Orleans-style dish.

Harvard Beets

makes 6 servings
ideal slow cooker: 3-quart

⅓ cup sugar
2 Tbsp. all-purpose flour
¼ cup beet juice or water
¼ cup white vinegar
2 16-oz. cans sliced beets, drained

1. Stir together sugar and flour.
Stir in beet juice and vinegar and
mix well.
2. Place beets in slow cooker. Pour
sugar and vinegar mixture over
beets. Stir to coat.
3. Cover and cook on high 1 hour.
Turn to low until ready to serve.

healthy for you

Asian Broccoli

makes 8 servings
ideal slow cooker: 3½- or 4-quart

2 lbs. fresh broccoli, trimmed and
    chopped into bite-size pieces
1 garlic clove, minced
1 green or red bell pepper, cut into
    thin slices
1 onion, cut into slices
¼ cup light soy sauce
½ tsp. salt
Dash of black pepper
1 Tbsp. sesame seeds (optional)

1. Combine all ingredients except
sesame seeds in slow cooker.
2. Cover and cook on low 6 hours.
Top with sesame seeds, if desired.
3. Serve over brown rice.

Doris' Broccoli and Cauliflower with Cheese

makes 8 servings
ideal slow cooker: 4-quart

1 lb. frozen cauliflower florets
2 10-oz. pkgs. frozen broccoli
   florets
½ cup water
2 cups shredded Cheddar cheese

1. Place cauliflower and broccoli in slow cooker.
2. Add water. Top with cheese.
3. Cover and cook on low 1½ to 3 hours, depending upon how crunchy or soft you want the vegetables.

---

editor's favorite

Corn Pudding

makes 3 to 4 servings
ideal slow cooker: 3-quart

2 eggs, beaten slightly
¼ cup sugar
1 tsp. salt
⅛ tsp. pepper
2 Tbsp. melted butter
2 Tbsp. all-purpose flour
½ cup milk
16-oz. can cream-style corn

1. Combine all ingredients except corn. Pour into slow cooker.
2. Add corn. Mix well.
3. Cover and cook on low 4 hours.

variation:

• Add ½ cup grated cheese to Step 2.

Golden Cauliflower

makes 4 to 6 servings
ideal slow cooker: 3-quart

2 10-oz. pkgs. frozen cauliflower
   florets, thawed
8-oz. jar cheese sauce
4 bacon slices, crisply browned and
   crumbled

1. Place cauliflower in slow cooker.
2. Pour cheese over top. Top with bacon.
3. Cover and cook on high 1½ hours and then on low 2 hours or cook only on low 4 to 5 hours.

---

entertaining

Caponata

makes 8 to 10 servings
ideal slow cooker: 4-quart

1 medium eggplant, peeled and
   cut into ½-inch cubes
14-oz. can diced tomatoes
1 medium onion, chopped
1 red bell pepper, cut into ½-inch
   pieces
¾ cup salsa
¼ cup olive oil
2 Tbsp. capers, drained
3 Tbsp. balsamic vinegar
3 garlic cloves, minced
1¼ tsp. dried oregano
⅓ cup chopped fresh basil, packed
   in measuring cup
Toasted, sliced French bread

1. Combine all ingredients except basil and bread in slow cooker.
2. Cover and cook on low 7 to 8 hours or until vegetables are tender.
3. Stir in basil. Serve on toasted bread.

---

healthy for you

Mexican Corn

makes 8 servings
ideal slow cooker: 3- or 4-quart

2 10-oz. pkgs. frozen whole-kernel
   corn, partially thawed
4-oz. jar chopped pimientos
⅓ cup chopped green bell pepper
⅓ cup water
1 tsp. salt
¼ tsp. black pepper
½ tsp. paprika
½ tsp. chili powder

1. Combine all ingredients in slow cooker.
2. Cover and cook on high 45 minutes and then on low 2 to 4 hours. Stir occasionally.

variation:

• For more fire, add ⅓ cup salsa and increase the pepper, paprika, and chili powder to match your taste.

Mushroom Stuffing

makes 7 to 8 cups
ideal slow cooker: 5-quart

1 cup finely chopped onion
1 cup finely chopped celery
½ cup butter or margarine
8-oz. can sliced mushrooms,
   drained
¼ cup chopped fresh parsley
1½ to 2 tsp. poultry seasoning,
   according to your taste
   preference
½ tsp. salt
⅛ tsp. pepper
12 cups toasted bread cubes
2 eggs, well beaten
1½ cups chicken broth

1. Sauté onion and celery in butter in skillet until cooked. Stir in mushrooms and parsley.
2. Combine seasonings and sprinkle over bread cubes.
3. Gently add remaining ingredients to bread cubes. Spoon lightly into slow cooker.
4. Cover and cook on high 1 hour and then on low 1 to 2 hours.

note:

: • This recipe is not as much a time-saver as it is a space-saver. If your oven is full, make your stuffing in your slow cooker.

Mediterranean Eggplant

makes 8 servings
ideal slow cooker: 5-quart

1 medium-size red onion, chopped
2 garlic cloves, crushed
1 cup fresh mushrooms, sliced
2 Tbsp. olive oil
1 eggplant, unpeeled and cubed
2 green bell peppers, coarsely chopped
28-oz. can crushed tomatoes, undrained
28-oz. can garbanzo beans, rinsed and drained
2 Tbsp. minced fresh rosemary
1 cup fresh parsley, chopped
½ cup kalamata olives, pitted and sliced

1. Spray slow cooker with cooking spray.
2. Sauté onion, garlic, and mushrooms in olive oil in a skillet over medium heat. Transfer to slow cooker.
3. Add eggplant, peppers, tomatoes, garbanzos, rosemary, and parsley.

4. Cover and cook on low 5 to 6 hours.
5. Stir in sliced olives just before serving.
6. Serve mixture with couscous or polenta.

Wild Mushrooms Italian

makes 5 to 7 servings
ideal slow cooker: 5-quart

2 large onions, chopped
3 large red bell peppers, chopped
3 large green bell peppers, chopped
2 Tbsp. oil
12-oz. pkg. oyster mushrooms, cleaned and chopped
4 garlic cloves, minced
3 bay leaves
10 fresh basil leaves, chopped
1½ tsp. salt
1½ tsp. black pepper
28-oz. can low-sodium Italian plum tomatoes, crushed or chopped

1. Sauté onion and bell peppers in oil in skillet until soft. Stir in mushrooms and garlic. Sauté just until mushrooms begin to turn brown. Pour into slow cooker.
2. Add remaining ingredients. Stir well.
3. Cover and cook on low 6 to 8 hours. Remove and discard bay leaves before serving.

note:

: • This dish is good as an appetizer on pita bread or served over rice or pasta for a main dish.

5 ingredients or less
Caramelized Onions

makes 8 servings
ideal slow cooker: 4-quart

6 large Vidalia or other sweet onions
4 Tbsp. margarine
10-oz. can chicken or vegetable broth

1. Peel onions. Remove stems and root ends. Place in slow cooker.
2. Pour margarine and broth over onions.
3. Cook on low 12 hours.

note:

: • Serve as a side dish, use onions and liquid to flavor soups or stews, or top a pizza.

Garlic Mashed Potatoes

makes 6 servings
ideal slow cooker: 4-quart

2 lbs. baking potatoes, unpeeled, cut in ½-inch cubes
¼ cup water
3 Tbsp. butter, sliced
1 tsp. salt
¾ tsp. garlic powder
¼ tsp. black pepper
1 cup milk

1. Combine all ingredients except milk in slow cooker. Toss to combine.
2. Cover and cook on high 4 hours or on low 7 hours.
3. Add milk to potatoes during last 30 minutes of cooking.
4. Mash potatoes with potato masher or electric mixer until fairly smooth.

Sweet Potato Casserole

makes 8 servings
ideal slow cooker: 3½-quart

2 28-oz. cans sweet potatoes, drained and mashed
2 Tbsp. brown sugar
1 Tbsp. orange juice
2 eggs, beaten

½ cup fat-free milk
⅓ cup chopped pecans
⅓ cup brown sugar
2 Tbsp. all-purpose flour
2 tsp. butter, melted

1. Combine sweet potatoes and 2 Tbsp. brown sugar.

2. Stir in orange juice, eggs, and milk. Place into greased slow cooker.

3. Combine pecans, ⅓ cup brown sugar, flour, and melted butter. Spread over sweet potatoes.

4. Cover and cook on high 3 to 4 hours.

healthy for you
Mustard Potatoes

makes 6 servings
ideal slow cooker: 4-quart

½ cup chopped onion
1 Tbsp. butter
1½ tsp. prepared mustard
1 tsp. salt
¼ tsp. pepper
½ cup fat-free or 2% milk
¼ lb. low-fat cheese
6 medium potatoes, cooked and
  grated

1. Sauté onion in butter in skillet.
Add mustard, salt, pepper, milk,
and cheese.
2. Place potatoes in slow cooker.
Do not press down.
3. Pour cheese mixture over
potatoes.
4. Cover and cook on low 3 to 4
hours.
5. Toss potatoes with a large spoon
when ready to serve.

note:

: • If you like a very mustardy
: taste, double the amount of
: mustard.

kid-friendly
Creamy Hash Browns

makes 14 servings
ideal slow cooker: 4- or 5-quart

2 lb. pkg. frozen cubed hash brown
  potatoes
2 cups cubed or shredded fat-free
  American cheese
12 oz. fat-free sour cream
10¾-oz. can cream of celery soup
10¾-oz. can 98% fat-free, lower-
  sodium cream of chicken soup
¼ lb. slices bacon, cooked and
  crumbled
1 medium onion, chopped
2 Tbsp. margarine, melted
¼ tsp. pepper

1. Place potatoes in slow cooker.
Combine remaining 8 ingredients
and pour over potatoes. Mix well.
2. Cover and cook on low 4 to 5
hours or until potatoes are tender.

Cheesy
Scalloped Potatoes

makes 7 servings
ideal slow cooker: 4- or 5-quart

2 lbs. potatoes, peeled and thinly
  sliced
1 cup water
½ tsp. cream of tartar
1 small onion, thinly sliced
¼ cup all-purpose flour
¼ tsp. garlic powder
¼ tsp. black pepper
2 Tbsp. low-sodium butter
10¾-oz. can 98% fat-free cream of
  mushroom soup
4 slices reduced-sodium American
  cheese

1. Toss potato slices in water and
cream of tartar. Drain.
2. Lay half of potatoes in slow
cooker sprayed with non-fat cooking spray.
3. Top with half each of the onion
slices, flour, garlic powder, and
pepper.
4. Add remaining potatoes and
onion. Sprinkle with remaining
flour, garlic powder, and pepper.
5. Add butter and soup.
6. Cover and cook on high 3 to 4
hours or on low 7 to 9 hours.
7. Garnish with cheese just before
serving.

Baked Acorn Squash

Baked Acorn Squash

makes 4 servings
ideal slow cooker: 6-quart oval

....

2 acorn squash
⅔ cup cracker crumbs
½ cup coarsely chopped pecans
⅓ cup butter or margarine, melted
¼ cup brown sugar
½ tsp. salt
¼ tsp. ground nutmeg
2 Tbsp. orange juice

1. Wash squash. Cut in half and remove seeds.
2. Combine remaining ingredients. Spoon into squash halves. Place squash in slow cooker.

3. Cover and cook on low 5 hours or until squash is tender.

Apple-Walnut Squash

makes 4 servings
ideal slow cooker: 3-quart

....

¼ cup water
2 small acorn squash
¼ cup firmly packed brown sugar
¼ cup butter, melted
3 Tbsp. apple juice
1½ tsp. ground cinnamon
¼ tsp. salt
1 cup toasted walnuts
1 apple, chopped

1. Pour water into slow cooker.
2. Cut squash in half crosswise. Remove seeds. Place in slow cooker, cut sides up.
3. Combine brown sugar, butter, apple juice, cinnamon, and salt. Spoon over squash.
4. Cover and cook on high 3 to 4 hours or until squash is tender.
5. Combine walnuts and chopped apple. Add to center of squash and mix with sauce to serve.
6. Serve with a pork dish.

Very Special Spinach

makes 8 servings
ideal slow cooker: 4-quart

3 10-oz. boxes frozen spinach,
  thawed and drained
2 cups 1% low-fat cottage cheese
1½ cups grated fat-free Cheddar
  cheese
3 eggs
¼ cup all-purpose flour
4 Tbsp. (¼ cup) light, soft tub
  margarine, melted

1. Mix together all ingredients.
2. Pour into slow cooker.
3. Cook on high 1 hour. Reduce
heat to low and cook 4 hours
more.

Orange Yams

makes 6 to 8 servings
ideal slow cooker: 4- or 5-quart

40-oz. can no-sugar-added yams,
  drained
2 apples, cored, peeled, and thinly
  sliced
1½ Tbsp. light, soft tub margarine,
  melted
2 tsp. orange zest
1 cup orange juice
2 Tbsp. cornstarch
¼ cup brown sugar
Brown sugar substitute to equal
  2 Tbsp.
1 tsp. salt
Dash of ground cinnamon and/or
  nutmeg

1. Place yams and apples in slow
cooker.
2. Add margarine and orange zest.
3. Combine remaining ingredients
and pour over yams.
4. Cover and cook on high 1 hour
and then on low 2 hours or until
apples are tender.

variation:

: • Substitute 6 to 8 medium-size
: cooked sweet potatoes or approx-
: imately 4 cups cubed butternut
: squash for yams.

Stewed Tomatoes

makes 10 to 12 servings
ideal slow cooker: 3- or 4-quart

2 qts. canned tomatoes
⅓ cup sugar
1½ tsp. salt
Dash of pepper
2 cups bread cubes
3 Tbsp. butter, melted

1. Place tomatoes in slow cooker.
2. Sprinkle with sugar, salt, and
pepper.
3. Lightly toss bread cubes
in melted butter. Spread over
tomatoes.
4. Cover and cook on high 3 to 4
hours.

Squash Medley

makes 8 servings
ideal slow cooker: 4-quart

8 summer squash, each about 4
  inches long, thinly sliced
½ tsp. salt
2 tomatoes, peeled and chopped
¼ cup sliced green onions
Half a small green bell pepper,
  chopped
1 chicken bouillon cube
¼ cup hot water
4 slices bacon, fried and crumbled
¼ cup fine dry bread crumbs

1. Sprinkle squash with salt.
2. Layer half the squash, tomatoes,
onion, and bell pepper in slow
cooker. Repeat layers.
3. Dissolve bouillon in hot water.
Pour into slow cooker.
4. Top with bacon. Sprinkle bread
crumbs over top.
5. Cover and cook on low 4 to 6
hours.

Ratatouille

Ratatouille

makes 6 servings
ideal slow cooker: 5- or 6-quart

1 Tbsp. olive oil
1 large onion, chopped
6 large garlic cloves, minced
1 green bell pepper, cut in strips
1 red bell pepper, cut in strips
1 medium eggplant, cubed
2 cups mushrooms, thickly sliced
4 tomatoes, cubed
1 cup low-sodium tomato puree
¼ cup dry red wine or wine vinegar
1 Tbsp. lemon juice
2 tsp. dried thyme
1 tsp. dried oregano
1 tsp. ground cumin
½ to 1 tsp. salt
¼ to ½ tsp. black pepper
4 Tbsp. minced fresh basil
¼ cup chopped fresh parsley
¼ cup grated fresh Parmesan
    cheese

1. Turn slow cooker on high for 2 minutes.
2. Pour oil into slow cooker and add remaining ingredients except fresh basil, parsley, and cheese.
3. Cover and cook on high 2 hours and then on low 4 to 5 hours.
4. Stir in fresh basil. Sprinkle with parsley and Parmesan cheese. Serve.

note:

: • This dish is delicious over
: whole wheat pasta or brown rice.

"Stir-Fry" Veggies

makes 8 servings
ideal slow cooker: 6-quart

16-oz. bag baby carrots
4 celery ribs, cut into chunks
1 medium onion, diced
14½-oz. can low-sodium Italian-
    style stewed tomatoes,
    undrained
½ tsp. dried basil
½ tsp. dried oregano
½ tsp. salt
1 large red or yellow bell pepper,
    diced
1 small head cabbage, chopped
1 lb. fresh broccoli, chopped

1. Combine carrots, celery, onion, tomatoes, basil, oregano, and salt in slow cooker.
2. Cover and cook on high 3 to 4 hours or on low 6 to 8 hours, stirring occasionally.
3. Stir in bell pepper, cabbage, and broccoli.
4. Cook on high 1 hour or on low 2 hours, stirring occasionally. You may need to add a little water if there is no liquid left on the veggies.

note:

: • Serve this as a side dish or as a
: main dish over hot cooked rice
: garnished with Parmesan cheese.

Herbed Lentils and Rice

makes 4 servings
ideal slow cooker: 3-quart

2¾ cups reduced-sodium, fat-free
    chicken broth
¾ cup water
¾ cup dry lentils, rinsed
¾ cup chopped onion
½ cup dry wild rice
½ tsp. dried basil
¼ tsp. dried oregano
¼ tsp. dried thyme
⅛ tsp. garlic powder
½ tsp. salt
¼ tsp. pepper
1 cup shredded reduced-fat Swiss
    cheese

1. Spray slow cooker with cooking
spray.
2. Combine all ingredients except
cheese in slow cooker.
3. Cover and cook on low 6 to 8
hours or until lentils and rice are
tender. Do not remove lid until
lentils and rice have cooked at
least 6 hours.
4. Stir in shredded cheese 5 to 10
minutes before serving.

Risi e Bisi (Rice and Peas)

makes 8 servings
ideal slow cooker: 4-quart

1½ cups converted long grain
    white rice, uncooked
¾ cup chopped onions
2 garlic cloves, minced
2 14½-oz. cans reduced-sodium
    chicken broth
⅓ cup water
¾ tsp. dried Italian seasoning
½ tsp. dried basil leaves
½ cup frozen baby peas, thawed
¼ cup freshly grated Parmesan
    cheese

1. Combine rice, onions, and garlic
in slow cooker.
2. In saucepan, stir together
chicken broth and water. Bring to
a boil. Add Italian seasoning and
basil leaves. Stir into rice mixture.
3. Cover and cook on low 2 to 3
hours or until liquid is absorbed.
4. Stir in peas. Cover and cook 30
minutes. Stir in cheese.

Herb Rice

makes 6 servings
ideal slow cooker: 3½-quart

pictured on page 136

3 chicken bouillon cubes
3 cups hot water
1½ cups uncooked long grain rice
1 tsp. dried rosemary
½ tsp. dried marjoram
¼ cup chopped fresh parsley
1 Tbsp. butter or margarine
¼ cup diced green onions
½ cup sliced almonds (optional)

1. Stir together chicken bouillon
cubes and water in slow cooker.
2. Add remaining ingredients
except almonds, if desired, in slow
cooker.
3. Cook on low 3½ to 4 hours or
until rice is fully cooked. Toss
with almonds before serving.

note:

• If you prefer, substitute 24 ozs.
(3 cups) fat-free low-sodium
chicken broth for the bouillon
cubes and water.

Old-Fashioned
Rice Pudding

sweets

15-minute prep
Old-Fashioned Rice Pudding

makes 8 servings
ideal slow cooker: 2½-quart

2 cups cooked white rice
1½ cups fat-free evaporated milk
⅓ cup brown sugar
2 Tbsp. margarine
2 tsp. vanilla extract
½ tsp. ground nutmeg
¾ cup fat-free, cholesterol-free egg product
1 cup raisins

1. Combine all ingredients in slow cooker sprayed with non-fat cooking spray.
2. Cover and cook on low 2½ hours, stirring every 30 minutes.

kid-friendly
Apple-Caramel Dessert

makes 7 servings
ideal slow cooker: 3-quart

½ cup apple juice
7 ozs. caramel candies
1 tsp. vanilla extract
⅛ tsp. ground cardamom
½ tsp. ground cinnamon
⅓ cup creamy peanut butter
2 medium apples, peeled, cored, and cut in wedges
7 slices angel food cake
1 qt. vanilla ice cream

1. Combine apple juice, caramel candies, vanilla, and spices. Place in slow cooker.
2. Drop peanut butter, 1 tsp. at a time, into slow cooker. Stir.
3. Add apple wedges.
4. Cover and cook on low 5 hours.
5. Stir well.
6. Cover and cook on low 1 hour more.
7. Serve ⅓ cup warm mixture over each slice of angel food cake and top with ice cream.

kid-friendly
Applescotch Crisp

makes 6 servings
ideal slow cooker: 3-quart

4 cups peeled and sliced cooking apples
⅔ cup brown sugar
½ cup all-purpose flour
½ cup quick-cooking oats
3.125-oz. pkg. butterscotch cook-n-serve pudding mix
1 tsp. ground cinnamon
½ cup cold butter or margarine

1. Place apples in slow cooker.
2. Combine sugar, flour, oats, pudding mix, and cinnamon. Cut in butter until mixture resembles coarse crumbs. Sprinkle over apples.
3. Cover and cook on low 5 to 6 hours.
4. Serve with ice cream.

note:

• For a less sweet dish, use only ¼ cup brown sugar.

Zesty Pears

makes 6 servings
ideal slow cooker: 3-quart

6 fresh pears
½ cup raisins
¼ cup brown sugar
1 tsp. grated lemon peel
¼ cup brandy
½ cup sweet white wine
½ cup macaroon crumbs

1. Peel and core pears. Cut into thin slices.
2. Combine raisins, sugar, and lemon peel. Layer alternately with pear slices in slow cooker.
3. Pour brandy and wine over top.
4. Cover and cook on low 4 to 6 hours.
5. Spoon into serving dishes. Cool. Sprinkle with macaroons. Serve plain or topped with sour cream.

Chocolate Rice Pudding

makes 4 serving
ideal slow cooker: 4-quart

4 cups cooked white rice
¾ cups sugar
¼ cup baking cocoa powder
3 Tbsp. butter, melted
1 tsp. vanilla extract
2 12-oz. cans evaporated milk
Whipped cream
Sliced toasted almonds
Maraschino cherries

1. Combine first 6 ingredients in greased slow cooker.
2. Cover and cook on low 2½ to 3½ hours or until liquid is absorbed.
3. Serve warm or chilled. Top individual servings with whipped cream, almonds, and cherries.

entertaining • for the holidays
Bread Pudding

makes 6 servings
ideal slow cooker: 5-quart

8 slices bread (raisin bread is especially good), cubed
4 eggs
2 cups milk
¼ cup sugar
¼ cup butter or margarine, melted
½ cup raisins (use only ¼ cup if using raisin bread)
½ tsp. ground cinnamon
Sauce:
2 Tbsp. butter or margarine
2 Tbsp. all-purpose flour
1 cup water
¾ cup sugar
1 tsp. vanilla extract

1. Place bread cubes in greased slow cooker.
2. Beat together eggs and milk. Stir in sugar, butter, raisins, and cinnamon. Pour over bread in slow cooker and stir.
3. Cover and cook on high 1 hour and then on low 3 to 4 hours or until thermometer inserted in bread pudding registers 160°.
4. Make sauce just before pudding is baked. Begin by melting butter in saucepan. Stir in flour until smooth. Gradually add water, sugar, and vanilla. Bring to a boil. Cook, stirring constantly 2 minutes or until thickened.
5. Serve sauce over warm bread pudding.

variation:

• Use dried cherries instead of raisins. Use cherry flavoring in sauce instead of vanilla.

Spoon Peaches

makes 6 servings
ideal slow cooker: 4-quart

⅓ cup granulated sugar
½ cup brown sugar
¾ cup buttermilk baking mix
2 eggs
2 tsp. vanilla extract
2 tsp. butter or margarine, melted
Half a 12-oz. can evaporated milk
2 cups mashed peaches, fresh, frozen, or canned (if canned, drain slightly)
¾ tsp. cinnamon

1. Combine granulated sugar, brown sugar, and baking mix in a bowl.
2. Add eggs and vanilla. Mix well.
3. Add margarine and milk. Mix well.
4. Add peaches and cinnamon. Mix well. Pour into greased slow cooker.
5. Cover and cook on low 6 to 8 hours.
6. Serve warm with whipped cream or vanilla ice cream.

make-ahead
Custard Rice Pudding

makes 4 to 6 servings
ideal slow cooker: 4- or 5-quart

¼ cup long grain white rice, uncooked
2 eggs
⅓ cup sugar
¼ tsp. salt
½ tsp. vanilla extract
1½ cups milk
⅓ cup raisins
Ground nutmeg or cinnamon
2 cups water

1. Cook rice according to package directions.
2. Beat together eggs, sugar, salt, vanilla, and milk. Stir in rice and raisins.
3. Pour into a 1-qt. baking dish that will fit into your slow cooker. Sprinkle with nutmeg.
4. Cover with aluminum foil and set on a metal trivet or a canning jar ring in bottom of slow cooker. Pour water around dish.
5. Cover and cook on high 2 to 2½ hours or until set.
6. Serve warm or chilled.

make-ahead
Mama's Rice Pudding

makes 8 servings
ideal slow cooker: 4-quart

½ cup long grain white rice, uncooked
⅓ cup sugar
1 tsp. vanilla extract
1 tsp. lemon extract
1 cup plus 2 Tbsp. fat-free milk
1 tsp. butter
2 eggs, beaten
1 tsp. ground cinnamon
½ cup raisins
1 cup fat-free whipping cream, whipped
Ground nutmeg

1. Combine all ingredients except whipped cream and nutmeg in slow cooker. Stir well.
2. Cover and cook on low 6 to 7 hours or until rice is tender and milk is absorbed, stirring once every 2 hours during cooking.
3. Pour into a bowl. Cover with plastic wrap and chill.
4. Before serving, fold in whipped cream and sprinkle with nutmeg.

Cherry Cobbler

Cherry Cobbler

makes 6 servings
ideal slow cooker: 3-quart

20-oz. can light cherry pie filling
1 cup all-purpose flour
¼ cup sugar
¼ cup butter, melted
½ cup fat-free milk
1½ tsp. baking powder
½ tsp. almond extract
¼ tsp. salt

1. Pour pie filling into greased slow cooker.
2. Combine remaining 7 ingredients. Beat until smooth. Spread over pie filling.
3. Cover and cook on high 2 hours.

note:

• Put the finishing touch on this juicy cobbler with a scoop of vanilla ice cream.

kid-friendly
Chocolate-Peanut Butter Cake

makes 11 servings
ideal slow cooker: 4-quart

2 cups (half an 18.25-oz. pkg.) milk chocolate cake mix
½ cup water
¼ cup peanut butter
1 egg
2 egg whites
6 Tbsp. chopped walnuts

1. Combine all ingredients. Beat 2 minutes with electric mixer.
2. Pour into greased and floured 3 lb. shortening can. Place can in slow cooker.
3. Cover top of can with 8 paper towels.
4. Cover and cook on high 2 to 3 hours.
5. Cool 10 minutes. Run knife around edge and invert cake onto serving plate. Cool completely before slicing and serving.

Date and Nut Loaf

makes 16 servings
ideal slow cooker: 4- or 5-quart

1½ cups boiling water
1½ cups chopped dates
1¼ cups sugar
1 egg
2 tsp. baking soda
½ tsp. salt
1 tsp. vanilla extract
1 Tbsp. melted butter
2½ cups all-purpose flour
1 cup walnuts, chopped
2 cups hot water

1. Pour 1½ cups boiling water over dates in medium bowl. Let stand 5 to 10 minutes.
2. Stir in sugar, egg, baking soda, salt, vanilla, and butter.
3. In separate bowl, combine flour and nuts. Stir into date mixture.
4. Pour into 2 greased 11.5-oz. coffee cans or 8-cup baking insert. If using coffee cans, cover with aluminum foil and tie. If using baking insert, cover with its lid. Place cans or insert on rack in slow cooker. (If you don't have a rack, use rubber jar rings instead.)
5. Pour 2 cups hot water around cans, up to half their height.
6. Cover and cook on high 3½ to 4 hours.
7. Remove cans or insert from cooker. Let bread stand in coffee cans or baking insert 10 minutes. Turn out onto cooling rack. Slice. Spread with butter, cream cheese, or peanut butter.

Fruit Medley

makes 6 to 8 servings
ideal slow cooker: 3-quart

Serve as a side dish, a dessert, or a topping for ice cream.

1½ lbs. mixed dried fruit
2½ cups water
1 cup sugar
1 Tbsp. honey
Peel of half a lemon, cut into thin strips
⅛ tsp. ground nutmeg
1 cinnamon stick
3 Tbsp. cornstarch
¼ cup cold water
¼ cup Cointreau

1. Place dried fruit in slow cooker. Pour in water.
2. Stir in sugar, honey, lemon peel, nutmeg, and cinnamon.
3. Cover and cook on low 2 to 3 hours. Turn cooker to high.
4. Stir together cornstarch and water until smooth. Stir into fruit mixture. Cook on high 10 minutes or until thickened.
5. Stir in Cointreau.
6. Serve warm or chilled.

Fruit Compote Dessert

makes 8 servings
ideal slow cooker: 4-quart

2 medium-size tart apples, peeled
2 medium-size fresh peaches, peeled and cubed
2 cups unsweetened pineapple chunks
1¼ cups unsweetened pineapple juice
¼ cup honey
2¼-inch thick lemon slices
3½-inch cinnamon stick
1 medium-size firm banana, thinly sliced
Whipped cream, sliced almonds, maraschino cherries (optional)

1. Cut apples into ¼-inch slices and then in half horizontally. Place in slow cooker.
2. Add peaches, pineapple, pineapple juice, honey, lemon, and cinnamon. Cover and cook on low 3 to 4 hours.
3. Stir in banana slices just before serving. Garnish with whipped cream, sliced almonds, and cherries, if desired.

Chocolate Mud Cake

makes 8 servings
ideal slow cooker: 3½- or 4-quart

1 cup all-purpose flour
2 tsp. baking powder
2 Tbsp. butter
2 ozs. semisweet chocolate or
⅓ cup semisweet chocolate
morsels
1 cup granulated sugar, divided
½ cup Dutch process cocoa, divided
1 Tbsp. vanilla extract
¼ tsp. salt
⅓ cup fat-free milk
1 egg yolk
⅓ cup brown sugar
1½ cups hot water
Vanilla ice cream (optional)

1. Spray slow cooker with cooking spray.
2. In a mixing bowl, whisk together flour and baking powder. Set aside.
3. In a large microwave-safe bowl, melt butter and chocolate in microwave at HIGH power for 40 seconds. Mix well.
4. Whisk ⅔ cup granulated sugar, 3 Tbsp. cocoa, vanilla, salt, milk, and egg yolk into chocolate mixture.
5. Add flour mixture. Stir until thoroughly mixed.
6. Pour batter into slow cooker. Spread evenly.

7. Whisk together remaining granulated sugar, remaining cocoa, brown sugar, and hot water until sugar is dissolved. Pour over batter in slow cooker. Do not stir.
8. Cover and cook on high 2 hours. The cake will be very moist and floating on a layer of molten chocolate when it's done. And you'll know it's done cooking when its edges begin to pull away from the sides of the insert and nearly all the cake is set.
9. Turn off slow cooker and remove lid. Try not to let the condensation from the lid drip onto the cake. Let cool for 25 minutes before spooning into individual bowls. Serve with vanilla ice cream, if desired.

Easy Chocolate Clusters

Easy Chocolate Clusters

makes 3½ dozen
ideal slow cooker: 3-quart

....

2 lbs. white chocolate coating,
    broken into small pieces
12-oz. pkg. semisweet chocolate
    morsels
4-oz. pkg. sweet German
    chocolate, chopped
24-oz. jar roasted peanuts

1. Combine chocolate coating,
chocolate morsels, and German
chocolate in slow cooker. Cover
and cook on high 1 hour and
then on low 1 more hour or until
chocolate is melted, stirring every
15 minutes.

2. Stir in peanuts. Mix well.
3. Drop by teaspoonfuls onto wax
paper. Let stand until set. Store at
room temperature.

5 ingredients or less

Pineapple Upside-Down Cake

makes 10 servings
ideal slow cooker: 4-quart

....

½ cup butter or margarine, melted
1 cup brown sugar
1 medium-sized can pineapple
    slices, drained, reserving juice
6 to 8 maraschino cherries
18.25-oz. yellow cake mix

1. Combine butter and brown
sugar. Spread over bottom of well-
greased slow cooker.
2. Add pineapple slices and place
cherries in the center of each slice.
3. Prepare cake according to package directions, using pineapple
juice for part of liquid. Spoon cake
batter into cooker over fruit.
4. Cover cooker with 2 tea towels
and then with its own lid. Cook
on high 1 hour and then on low 3
to 4 hours.
5. Cool for 10 minutes. Then run
knife around edge and invert cake
onto large platter.

Creamy Orange Cheesecake

makes 10 servings
ideal slow cooker: 3-quart

Crust:

¾ cup graham cracker crumbs

2 Tbsp. sugar

3 Tbsp. melted butter

Filling:

2 8-oz. pkgs. cream cheese, at room temperature

⅔ cup sugar

2 eggs

1 egg yolk

¼ cup frozen orange juice concentrate

1 tsp. orange zest

1 Tbsp. all-purpose flour

½ tsp. vanilla extract

1. Combine crust ingredients. Pat into 7- or 9-inch springform pan, whichever size fits into your slow cooker.
2. Cream together cream cheese and sugar. Add eggs and yolk. Beat for 3 minutes.
3. Beat in juice, zest, flour, and vanilla. Beat 2 minutes. Pour batter into crust. Place on rack in slow cooker.
4. Cover and cook on high 2½ to 3 hours. Turn off and leave standing 1 to 2 hours or until cool enough to remove from cooker.
5. Cool completely before removing sides of pan. Chill before serving.
6. Serve with thawed frozen whipped topping and fresh or mandarin orange slices.

Graham Cracker Cookies

kid-friendly • make-ahead

makes 2½ dozen
ideal slow cooker: 4-quart

This fudgelike cookie is a family favorite. The slow cooker melts a large amount of chocolate and keeps the mixture warm while batches of cookies bake. Store cookies at room temperature in an airtight container.

12-oz. pkg. semisweet chocolate morsels

2 1-oz. squares unsweetened baking chocolate, shaved

2 14-oz. cans fat-free sweetened condensed milk

3 cups crushed graham cracker crumbs

1 cup finely chopped walnuts

1. Place chocolates in slow cooker.
2. Cover and cook on high 1 hour, stirring every 15 minutes. Continue to cook on low, stirring every 15 minutes or until chocolate is melted (about 30 minutes).
3. Stir milk into melted chocolate.
4. Add graham cracker crumbs, 1 cup at a time, stirring after each addition.
5. Stir in nuts (mixture should be thick but not stiff).
6. Drop by heaping teaspoonfuls onto lightly greased cookie sheets. Keep remaining mixture warm by covering and turning the slow cooker to warm.
7. Bake at 350° for 13 to 15 minutes or until tops of cookies begin to crack. Remove from oven. Cool 1 to 2 minutes before transferring to wax paper.

Graham Cracker Cookies

index